A Sprat to Catch a Mackerel

Key Principles to Build Your Business

Raymond Ackerman

with
Pippa de Bruyn and
Suzanne Ackerman

Jonathan Ball Publishers
Johannesburg & Cape Town

Published in trade paperback in 2010 by
JONATHAN BALL PUBLISHERS (PTY) LTD
PO Box 33977
Jeppestown
2043

ISBN 978-1-86842-369-9

Cover design by publicide, Durban
Text design by Triple M Design, Johannesburg
Set in 10.5/14 pt Rotis Serif Std
Printed and bound by CTP Book Printers, Cape

CONTENTS

DEDICATED TO ALL THOSE
EXTRAORDINARY HUMAN BEINGS
WHO CREATE JOBS, GROW THE ECONOMY AND
SERVE THEIR CUSTOMERS, WHILE LEADING
THE INDEPENDENT LIFE THEY'VE
ALWAYS DREAMED OF.

TO YOU, THE ENTREPRENEUR.

Prologue

Why I Decided to Write this Book

I never thought of myself as an entrepreneur. If I had not been fired from what I thought was a secure job in a large corporation, I would never have started my own business. Now it seems inconceivable that I might have been an employee my entire life, but I may very well have been seduced by the comforts of a steady monthly income and company benefits. It is a sobering thought, when you consider how many more entrepreneurs may remain trapped in jobs that grind their self-esteem and joy because they think they don't have what it takes – courage, money, particular skills, a business plan – to get a business off the ground.

I have written this book for those entrepreneurs 'in waiting', as well as those who already have a business up and running but are struggling to generate a viable income. In fact, anyone looking to enjoy greater satisfaction in their working environment will hopefully find some guidance in the following pages. Because as I sit here on the eve of my retirement, almost forty-five years after I bought my first four Pick 'n Pay stores, I can honestly say it has been an exhilarating ride. Being an entrepreneur enabled me to set in motion everything I ever wanted to achieve – the freedom to grow a business based on my personal principles, the ability to create jobs, tackle iniquitous cartels, break price monopolies and increase the country's tax base. And of course, to serve the South African consumer – my *primum movens*, the primary reason I wanted to create my own retail business. Because, aside from anything else, the entrepreneur essentially provides something that soc.... needs – something that makes the customer happy.

I am a fierce supporter of the entrepreneurial spirit, the lifeblood of a nation's economy. As such, I have always had an open-door policy for any student wanting advice on the business they want to get into, or for struggling entrepreneurs wondering where they've gone wrong. It's also why I founded my Academy of Entrepreneurial Development, a six-month, full-time programme offered to 18- to 30-year-olds from disadvantaged backgrounds, running at the UCT Graduate School of Business and the University of Johannesburg. Places are limited, however, and usually oversubscribed. So, when Jeremy Boraine of Jonathan Ball Publishers approached me about writing a book that would sum up my business philosophy in a simple, accessible way – one that would be relevant to anyone starting or trying to grow any kind of enterprise – I was persuaded that it could perhaps be useful to write one more book.

A Sprat to Catch a Mackerel is an encapsulation of my heartfelt belief in how small, seemingly insignificant actions – a chance meeting, a courteous gesture, an intense conversation, a keen observation, a systematic analysis, a positive response – can capture a big idea. Capture enough of them, and you build a great business. The most important events in life are sometimes the least predictable, but it's your attitude to these events that you can control. As such, this is not so much a 'how to' book as a summation of the principles and insights that I have gathered and developed over the years, and used to grow my own business organically. It is my humble hope that the broad-brush-stroke guidance provided in the following pages may in some way inspire a new generation of men and women, not only to achieve meaningful growth in your own business and life, but also to choose to support only the businesses that care about you the customer, their staff and the wider community.

The future is yours; serve it well.

CHAPTER 1

Passion – The Most Vital Ingredient of All

Deciding What to Do

PRINCIPLE #1

'Find meaning in life by doing the work you want to do, and do it to distraction.' – Dr Viktor Frankl

Choosing a business is a little like choosing a life partner. It doesn't matter whether you're a young student trying to carve out a future, a seasoned businessman unhappy with his lot, or recently fired from a job you may even have cared a great deal about: Starting your own business is not something you rush into, or take lightly. It has to be more than just vaguely suitable, or the first thing that comes up. Owning a business is relentless. No matter how successful you become, as the owner you can't ever rest up and say, 'I've made it'. So, in the end, the essential difference between the success and failure of an enterprise is the level of passion you bring to it. If you're not sure what kind of enterprise – or whether in fact any – could ignite this in you, it's worth sitting down and first doing a little mental research. Not only will it save you a great deal of money, but you won't waste your most precious commodity: time.

Your *interests* and *knowledge* are both terribly important. If you're fascinated by something, you will know a great deal about it. So hobbies – the things you do for pleasure in downtime – could be an important source. Alternatively, and usually more pertinent, is what you've been doing for a living.

Most successful entrepreneurs are people who launch businesses in the field they were employed in. I fully subscribe to Malcolm Gladwell's '10 000-hour rule', which essentially states that the key to real success in any field is a matter of practising a specific task for a total of around 10 000 hours! You can't put a price on the hours spent immersed in a particular environment, learning how a business works, the pitfalls and how and where it could be improved upon. Having worked in a certain industry, you will naturally also know your way around the feeder industries that surround it. Most importantly, the mistakes you make will be at someone else's expense. This is not a dishonest strategy. You are not using the company you are working for any more than they are using you and your skills to advance their profit. You get to hone your talents, while – all things being equal – your employer harnesses them to make more money: a fair trade

> '*Starting your own business is not something you rush into, or take lightly. It has to be more than just vaguely suitable, or the first thing that comes up.*'

in anyone's language. That's not to say it is not possible to strike out in an entirely fresh direction from your current career path and achieve long-term success, but your passion will need to be all the stronger to overcome the mistakes you will inevitably make in a brand-new industry.

At this stage, it may still not be clear to you exactly which route to take; not only whether to start your own business or not, but which industry to sink your savings and energy into. You may be toying with a variety of options, none of which jump out as '*the one*'. The following method should help you achieve clarity. You may find it rather simplistic, but it worked for me after I found myself jobless with a pregnant wife and three children to support, and it has worked for countless others who have asked me to help them find their feet in the four decades since I found mine. All you need are a few pieces of paper, a pen and the brutal honesty to explore every option.

The first step is to ask yourself, very clearly: *Do I really want to change my life?*

If the answer is a resounding yes, the next question is: *What* exactly *is the problem?*

Often, people strike out in a new direction, eager to escape what they perceive to be a trapped existence, but do not deal with the actual root of the problem. They then find them-selves in a new environment but feel the same desperation. So it's vitally important to clarify and distil what the *real* problem is.

Don't confuse the problem with the cause. This is a com-mon mistake, given that the cause is usually the thing more keenly felt. So 'I hate my job' could either be a problem, or it could be a cause, with the *real* problem lying deeper – for instance, 'I don't like the way my boss treats me' or 'I hate the fact that it keeps me from my family' or 'I'm not paid enough'.

Ask yourself: *Is it the broader career choice I have made,*

> *'Do not allow your inner critic to interfere while compiling a list of all the things you want to do before you die. This is not the time to self-edit.'*

or the particular job I am currently in? Is it really the job, or is it the people I am working with, or for? Is it perhaps my lifestyle? Is it affecting my health? Or does the real problem lie with my relationships at home? Try to cover all bases.

Having determined the root of the problem, you can now list the causes. There may be one, but more often than not there are four or five. Write them all down. If there is more than one problem, do a separate 'cause' analysis for each.

Having determined which aspect of your life you find most problematic, and clarified the causes, set these aside. It's time to move closer to the solution.

Take a fresh sheet of paper and write a list of all the things you have ever wanted to do before you die. Do not allow your 'inner critic' to interfere while compiling this list; this is not the time to self-edit. List even the crazy things, like jumping off a mountain strapped to a glider, or the idealistic dreams, like campaigning for environmental issues. Ask yourself: *What is it I want to achieve with my life? What do I want to spend all those working hours on? What will I regret not doing if I don't? What would be meaningful to me? What do I want to be remembered for?* Call it your 'Before I Kick the Bucket' list, and make it as long as you want.

When you're satisfied that you've listed all the things you

would really like to do, give each listed item a score out of 10, with 1 showing the lowest-level interest, and 10 being a sky-high-absolutely-must-do rating. Having given yourself free reign in the original listing, you may now allow realism to temper the actual scores.

Consider all factors. It's all very well wanting to make a living as an artist, for instance, but if you've never picked up a paintbrush you're unlikely to earn much, at least for a while. In my case, I always dreamed of being a doctor, but with a wife and children to support I did not have the luxury of time to pursue an eight-year degree, so, despite it being a long-held dream, I scored this a relatively low 3.

Now look at the list. How did you score 'Start my own business'?

Back in 1966 I gave this an 8. All the rest – emigrate, study further, join another company, and so on – scored 5 and under. As I looked at that piece of paper, I knew what my objective was. It was not only realistic and achievable, but also exhilarating. (As for jumping off a mountain, I finally got round to doing *that* aged 77, and it's something of a relief not to have to do it ever again!)

CHAPTER 2

Analysis – The First Part of Every Plan

How to Create a Business Plan

PRINCIPLE #2

'When in doubt, rely on the
"7 Tried & True" – what, where, why,
when, which, how and who.'

Entrepreneurs are neither born nor made. You may have certain innate instincts that will incline you towards entrepreneurial enterprise, but, frankly, a lot depends on outside influences, and how you choose to respond to them. Certainly, if you are the kind of person who constantly challenges the status quo in your working environment, and constantly looks for better, more efficient ways of doing things – be it working conditions, service delivery or manufacturing processes – then you have what is probably the key characteristic of a good entrepreneur. This is the 'vision' that people always refer to when talking about entrepreneurs: not just the ability to save or make more money, but to keep looking at new ways of doing things and finding alternate ways to give people what they need.

As a boy, I was shy and retiring, and was constantly warned by my father – a man of Victorian principles – that I was too kind, too nice, too worried about others to ever make a success of it. My small achievements at school – doing well academically, being chosen as a prefect, playing first team rugby – went largely ignored. It hurt me deeply that he refused to come and watch me play rugby. 'I'll come when you play for the Springboks,' he would say. But as a result of his impossibly high standards, I kept raising my own. I am by nature a team player, but in order to impress my father I was driven to achieve pole position in everything I tackled, and this internal pressure became a bit of a habit.

Still, it never occurred to me that I might be an entrepreneur. The general thinking – then as now – was that it was 'too late', that it had been somehow 'easier' during some earlier Arcadian era.

Soon after graduating, I joined Greatermans in Johannesburg on the advice of my father, whose aversion to debt had forced him to sell his own company, Ackermans, to the very consciously named Greatermans, where he now worked in what he himself regarded as the 'third team'. I remained a

'Entrepreneurs are neither born nor made.'

loyal employee at Greatermans for twelve years. My father passed away; I slowly climbed the ranks, reasonably content with earning my monthly stipend. I would probably never have started my own business if Greatermans had not taken the first step for me, and fired me.

Dealing with these two difficulties – trying to impress my authoritarian, difficult-to-please father, then the visionless, impossible-to-please company elders – was what 'nurtured' my entrepreneurial career. Both were problems I overcame by refusing to accept their version of me, and by analysing every situation in a kind of mental hopscotch that went 'Problem–Cause–Solution'.

In Chapter 1, I dealt with the importance of clarity, self-awareness and honesty when asking yourself, 'What *exactly* is the problem?', and, having identified the real root, listing its causes. But Problem–Cause–Solution analysis is just the initial step. Having identified the problem and its causes, and rated the possible solutions, the next step is to use the '7 Tried & True', asking yourself: what, where, why, when, which, how and who.

I used the '7 Tried & True' analysis to provide me with the logical, systematic steps I needed to realise the goal of starting my own business; indeed, it became the basis of my mission statement and my business plan. It focused me on where to shop for my business, what kind of business I was looking for, how I was going to achieve it, and so on. Over the years, I have encouraged many budding entrepreneurs to use the same simple tool as a basis for their own business plan. As in Chapter 1, all you need is a few sheets of paper, a pen and a few uninterrupted hours to work through the answers to the following questions:

> 1. **What** *type of enterprise would I be good at/would make me happy? What do I want to achieve in the short term/long term? What are the possible pitfalls/opportunities/etc?* This should have been somewhat clarified by the exercise in Chapter 1. This is also the place to visualise the worst things that could go wrong: **What** *would happen if I lost my health/there was a terrorist attack/a competitor opened next door ...* This is

not meant to deter you but to prepare you mentally for every eventuality.

2. Where *would I like to open my business/is there a need for my service or product/am I prepared to travel to/is the ideal place to bring up a family?*

3. Why *am/should I be doing this/is this a product or service that someone will be interested in purchasing or hiring/is there a gap?* List all the reasons here; again, this should have been clarified by the Chapter 1 exercise. If it evokes more than one answer, list them all and then score them out of 10 to ascertain the primary reason you want to launch this enterprise, and use this as the basis for your mission statement, after reading Chapter 3.

4. When *should I start?* Think about any specific event that will benefit you or your launch, or events in your personal calendar that may hinder or benefit you.

5. Which *format/kind of business/model fits best with my long-term plans?* Should I buy an existing business or start from scratch? Form a partnership or find shareholders?

6. How *do I research existing services or products for purposes of comparison/will my proposed* *enterprise operate logistically/will I finance my plan/will I promote my service or product/will I plan should things go wrong?*

7. Who *will be my customers/my employees/my accountant/my lawyer/my banker?*

PRINCIPLE #3

'If there's no solution, there's no problem.'

Aside from using the '7 Tried & True' analysis to help launch my business, I must briefly add here that it has been an immensely useful problem-solving process over the years. I extrapolate a little in Chapter 19 on what some like to call 'scenario planning'. I never had a name for it, but the desire to work through problems by looking at every possible angle has always been there, guided by the twin combination of curiosity and fear.

I have to admit to an almost pathological fear of failure. Regardless of how successful my business became, and how many good people I had in place looking after it, I found it almost impossible not to worry about it, like a slightly anx-

'I never ignored or dismissed my concerns as being over-anxious. I saw it as an ability to identify problems before they happen.'

ious parent, always keeping a watchful eye on their child, regardless of its age.

I never ignored or dismissed my concerns as being neurotic or over-anxious. I saw it as an ability to identify problems almost before they happen – not because I was some kind of visionary, but because I had the self-awareness to listen to the inner voice we all have which tells us when we are stepping close to danger. It's a voice that may wake you at night, or whisper to you while you shave, take the dog for a walk or play a round of golf. Ignore it at your peril.

Take out your pen, get a large piece of paper, and do the Problem–Cause–Solution mental hopscotch, then rate the solutions out of 10 as discussed in Chapter 1. Follow this initial analysis with the more in-depth '7 Tried & True' analysis. Not only will it help you navigate your way through any problem, but the very process will help set your mind at rest, allowing you to focus on the many other issues clamouring for your time as you set sail into the unknown.

CHAPTER 3

The Real Reason You're in Business

Developing a Mission Statement

PRINCIPLE #4

'Profits are the reward, not the reason, for being in business.'

A clearly defined mission statement is vital to even the smallest business – not just at the start (though never is clarity more essential) but also in the growth years to come. You will come to rely heavily on your mission statement to maintain focus and guide your endeavour.

Once your business is established, do not be tempted to change your mission statement. New blood, such as an ambitious MD, or a hot-shot ad agency eager to impress, may urge you to change it for what appear to be valid reasons (expanding product range, evolving population, keeping up with the times, and so on), but you do so at considerable risk. You may choose to elaborate on it over the years, but your first mission statement should be a short phrase – the shorter the better – that encapsulates a single value and homes in on one essential goal that everyone can relate to, allowing it to permeate every aspect of the company. In effect, your mission statement encapsulates the reason you are in business.

So, just *why* are you in business?

Most of us start our careers with the primary need to make money. We think money is the main reason we go to work – and heaven knows we certainly need it. But this soon starts to change. If money remains your primary motivation, you will, in the long run, have zero job satisfaction. You will become bored and demotivated, and life will be on hold until the after-work hours. If it was truly all about the money you could cheat or steal, but there is little pleasure in either – just as in a dead-end job. Even entrepreneurs who have started their businesses, but for the wrong reasons, will come to hate the relentless daily grind. At some point, we all realise that – important as it is – it's not really about the money.

There is no rule that says you can't change tack. Life is too short to spend the better part of it stuck in a hole-in-the-wall existence. If a business doesn't suit you, get out, and start again. But what will be the purpose of your next endeavour?

I can still recall the ripple of disbelief among the class of 1949 UCT commerce students when our lecturer, Professor WH Hutt, opened the lesson with these words: 'Most of you are here to make money, but you won't. Not unless you have a moral mission.' It was a shocking thing to say to a class of commerce students. Morality was a subject for arts students, not for those who had by choice of degree virtually stated the financial nature of their ambition. The majority of students thought he was talking rubbish. None of us in that classroom, including the professor himself, knew he would in later years be heralded as 'Economist of the Century' by the *Wall Street Journal*. But his revolutionary case for moral-obligation-as-business-principle struck a chord with me. I had given up my real ambition to study medicine in order to follow in the footsteps of my father and grandfather, both of whom were deeply entrenched in the retail industry. This decision

'Life is too short to spend the better part of it stuck in a hole-in-the-wall existence. If a business doesn't suit you, get out, and start again.'

was finally vindicated by Hutt's alluring suggestion that one could combine a deep-seated desire to serve humanity in some meaningful way with an interest in commerce, and that 'consumer sovereignty' was both sound business principle and moral duty.

Serendipitously, a few years later I was inspired by almost the exact same sentiments, this time from a dynamic, hard-bitten American retail genius. Bernard Trujillo, known in the 1950s as the 'Pope of modern marketing', espoused the concept of 'enlightened self-interest', according to which a business that showed real interest and concern for its consumers would in turn gain their loyalty, and their money. Providing goods at low prices was not about making money, or managing a balance sheet, but about meeting the very real needs of all consumers, particularly in the postwar years. Trujillo argued that the real driving force behind the rise of the big US supermarket was the Great Depression of the 1930s, when many Americans were literally starving. The primary incentive behind the innovations developed by retailers at the time was to alleviate the desperation of their fellow Americans. It was a moral imperative to drive down food prices because people were suffering; it would not have happened, or certainly not as fast, without that crushing consumer need.

Sitting there listening to Trujillo for the first time, I felt an acute kinship with his philosophy. The iniquity of so many South Africans living below the breadline, paying inflated prices for basic food commodities due to the existence of price monopolies, was a battle waiting to be fought. These people were entirely powerless. I, by contrast, with my privileged upbringing and status, could fight for their right to have food at realistic prices. Championing the consumer became my burning ambition, and when I started Pick 'n Pay a few years later my mission statement was simply 'consumer sovereignty' (which I will discuss in more detail in Chapter 11). It was the primary reason I went into business, and the reason I stayed in business.

This, in short, is how I came to develop my mission statement. Yours will be an amalgamation of your own life experiences, and will come primarily from a distillation of the answers to Question 3 of the '7 Tried & True' (see Chapter 2). But whatever the service or product, the core concept of most good mission statements will somehow be about serving your customer's needs better. This could be because you are offering an entirely new product or service, or a superior quality product or service, or the same but at a lower price, or simply a new, more streamlined way of doing things. Or it could be because your business is more conveniently located, or offers a more modern, exciting environment, or offers that elusive 'added value', and so on. But in essence, any successful business will always somehow encompass the sentiment: 'to better serve the customer'. The trick is how to maintain this, without the competition catching up.

PRINCIPLE #5

'Focus on a pinhead.'

I know there are many people who are capable of doing lots of different things, but for me focus is cardinal to success.

Having chosen what you want to do, dedicate yourself to doing this to the best of your abilities. Do not be distracted from your core business, at least initially. The more successful you become, the more people will demand your attention and your resources, encouraging you to spread yourself further and invest in their ideas.

Do not waver.

Having devised your mission statement (your primary reason for being in business, the answer that relates to the original question, 'What do I want to do with my life?'), place it at the very centre of your business, literally weaving it into every one of the Four Legs of the Table we will build in the next chapter. In this way you will be reminded that each of the Four Legs must always aid, support and answer the mission statement. If you are faced with a difficult decision or choice in any of the Four Legs, or have to choose between growth and control of the company, the final question will always be: *which decision will, in the long run, better serve my mission statement?*

Over the years, I was often faced with suggestions regarding a business development that would almost certainly

'If the solution serves the mission statement, and you can still see your way clear to a profit, this is the right route. Even if it costs more.'

turn a profit. However, if it did not fit my original mission statement – 'customer sovereignty' or serving my customers with the best produce at the lowest prices – it didn't fly. Keeping gross margins down as low as we do affects our profitability, but it is true to our mission statement, so we maintain them. In short, *even if it may cost more,* if the solution serves the mission statement, and you can still see your way clear to a profit, this is always the right route to take.

In conclusion, then, if your mission statement gives the consumer something he or she needs, and you ensure that it is a cardinal part of every decision you make, you *will* make money – just how much will depend on your ministering equally to the Four Legs of the Table.

CHAPTER 4

Building Four Balanced Legs for Your Table

A Business Model that Really Works

PRINCIPLE #6

'Success cannot be pursued, but ensues.' – Dr Viktor Frankl

Do not be concerned if you are not bursting with self-confidence. Many budding entrepreneurs with bright ideas simply lack the knowledge of how to implement them successfully. More important than confidence is self-awareness and self-honesty, and the methodology to apply these qualities successfully.

I have the following sign outside my door:

HOW TO SUCCEED

1) SET REASONABLE AND WORTHWHILE GOALS

2) WORK SYSTEMATICALLY TOWARDS ACHIEVING THOSE GOALS

3) MEASURE YOUR PERFORMANCE REGULARLY

Using the simple process of analysis described in the previous chapters, we have taken care of Step 1: setting reasonable and worthwhile goals. Now we need to work on your delivery.

Steps 2 and 3 are well serviced if you look at your business as a table supported by four legs. This is the business model

'Most entrepreneurs are too busy or just not particularly interested in administrative detail. If this is you, ensure you have help from the outset.'

that built Pick 'n Pay, and I describe in detail how I applied it to my business in my second book, *The Four Legs of the Table*. If you are in the retail industry it may be worth your while to refer to the book; if you have already read it, you can either recap here with this brief overview, or skip to the next chapter.

In essence, the Four Legs is a simple, foolproof model that can be successfully applied to absolutely any business. I have explained the principles of this model to a wide cross section of people, from young start-ups incubating their business plan to the surviving-but-struggling entrepreneur. Without fail, balancing the Four Legs has dramatically improved their business capacity and, ultimately, their turnover.

In brief, the concept of the Four Legs refers to the four pillars that support the tabletop that is your business. Balanced on the tabletop is your customer (be it a consumer, client, patient, etc). If the table is steady and strong, you will have a satisfied customer, blissfully unaware of the enormous amount of work that goes into keeping the table sturdy. But if it wobbles, you will have an unhappy customer, and your business will be heading for trouble.

The Four Legs – interdependent, depending on each other to support your business – are:

1. Administration (everything from stocktaking to accounting)

2. Merchandise (the product(s) or services offered)

3. PR/Social Responsibility/Marketing (the community you serve)

4. People (your employees)

The Four Legs are the three-dimensional shape you give the business plan you created with the '7 Tried & True' – they literally rise up from the paper analysis you completed in Chapters 1 and 2. You need to study each leg carefully so that you know how to build (and have budgeted for) a sturdy table on which your customer can be carried. To simplify the process, administer the '7 Tried & True' analysis to each Leg. In this way, while looking at how to build the first Leg (Administration), you would ask yourself the following kinds of questions:

1. What *kind of business entity should I create? (Pty Ltd, CC, sole proprietor, Trust?)* **What** *kind of administration do I need/feel comfortable with setting up/services do I need (in-house/work-from-home book-keeper; freelance accountant; established accounting firm?)* **What** *can I budget* *for this person/service?*

2. Where *will administration take place (in-house/outsourced/full-time/part-time/at home)?* **Where** *will I find the capital?*

3. Why *do I need to budget for this (manage cash flow/salaries/tax/wastage/monitor supplier and customer relationships etc)?*

4. When *should I pay attention to this/outsource it/hire someone?*

5. Which *computer system/model will deliver the kind of result I am looking for?*

6. How *much will I need to be involved/will it cost?* **How** *will I remember to get all the monthly SARS paperwork done in time?* **How** *will I control shrinkage?* **How** *can I reduce expenses?*

7. Who *should I approach to help me find the right person?*

To build the second Leg (Merchandise/Service), you could ask:

1. What *kind of product/service am I going to supply?* **What** *will differentiate it from my competitors?*

2. Where *will I find it/create it/offer it?*

3. Why *am I going to make money offering this kind of product/service?*

4. When *should I start purchasing/selling?*

5. Which *products/services should I offer?* Which *competitor offers anything similar?* Which *will be my loss-making lines (to pull in new customers) and my profit-generating items/services?*

6. How *much stock will I need to carry/budget for?* How *will I work out prices/control shrinkage?* How *will I keep innovating?* How *can I negotiate a lower price from suppliers?* How *will I cope with a price war/recession/terrorist attack?*

7. Who *will design the store/manage the stock?*

To build the third Leg (PR/Promotions), you could ask:

1. What *kind of PR or marketing am I going to do?* What *kind of community involvement am I interested in/is relevant to my business?* What *size should the budget be?*

2. Where *will I promote my business? Newspapers/ radio/magazines or other above-the-line media, and/or 'new' media (Facebook/Twitter/blog/website)? Billboards/vehicle or other signage?*

3. Why *do I want to use a particular medium/ spokesperson/tone of voice/etc?*

4. When *should I plan to advertise?*

5. Which *media will I use to promote my business?* Which *products/services will I concentrate on?* Which *community needs will I service?*

6. How *will I communicate with the public?* How *often?* How *wide/narrow should my communication focus be?* How *will I fund this?* How *can I find innovative ways to promote my business without blowing the budget?* How *can I live my public relations/develop a relationship with the press?*

7. Who *will conceive/design my signage/logo/ website/advertising?* Who *will advise on media placement or PR opportunities?*

To build the fourth Leg (People/Employees), you could ask:

1. What *kind of people am I looking for?* (Create a list of employees you think you need. Define the kind of personality for each, as well as the ideal qualifications and/or work experience of each person you intend hiring.) *Am I prepared to take on inexperienced enthusiasts or do I want people with a proven track record, or a mix?* What *kind of benefits (pension, medical, etc) will I offer?*

2. Where *will I find them? Through a recruitment agency? Adverts in specialist publications or general newspapers? Head-hunted from competitors?*

3. Why *am I looking for a particular kind of person? Are employees so important to my business?* **Why** *is it important to understand more about the BEE scorecard and how that differs from a company profile?* **Why** *do I need to be familiar with the Department of Trade & Industry's Code of Good Practice, and the SARS PAYE, UIF and SDL requirements?*

4. When *should I start looking? Before or after I have found the right premises? Within or without?*

5. Which *system of motivation/appreciation will deliver the kind of result I am looking for?*

6. How *many people will I need? Can I get away with less?* **How** *much will I need to budget for?* **How** *will I keep them motivated and involved?* **How** *will I ensure that I remain in contact with each employee/ensure that they feel heard?* **How** *will I discipline/fire my employees?*

7. Who *should I approach to help me with my HR queries?*

I cannot emphasise enough how vital it is that each of the Four Legs is seen to be of equal import, and therefore given equal attention. If you do not look after each Leg rigorously, one (or more) will atrophy, and your business will start to wobble out of control.

That said, balancing all Four Legs is not an easy task,

> *'Self-awareness is more useful than self-esteem.'*

given that there will be at least one area that you don't enjoy, don't feel confident about or are simply ill-equipped to handle – no one has *all* the characteristics needed to be strong in every Leg.

I knew from the outset that my weakest Leg was Administration, and this is usually the Leg that suffers most, particularly in a small business. Most entrepreneurs are too busy or just not particularly interested in that level of detail. If this is you, ensure you have help here from the outset. Similarly so, despite twelve years' retail experience I knew my merchandise knowledge was insufficient for the kind of operation I wanted. I needed an experienced buyer to deal with this crucial side of the business, so I hired the best person for this job.

Measure your abilities against each Leg in turn. This is where self-awareness is so much more useful than self-esteem! Having identified your weaknesses in any of the Legs, address them immediately – and make sure you budget for the help you need to balance the Table before you start out. Consider hiring the services of a PR expert if media or marketing is not your area of expertise (though there are many simple, cost-effective ways of reaching parts of your community, as discussed in Chapter 16). Or, if you struggle to remain positive when dealing with people (discussed in Chapter 17), invest in a human resources appointment, or a client liaison person to deal with customers. Hire an experienced buyer if you know nothing about merchandising. But, most crucially, hire a good accountant or book-keeper; the requirements from SARS alone can be extremely tedious.

Having launched your business with Four Legs that are sturdy and balanced, the next step is to keep measuring the strength of each Leg. Working systematically towards achieving your goals is in some ways the easy part – the tricky bit is to keep measuring performance.

PRINCIPLE #7

'Delegate does not mean abdicate.'

Hiring experts to help you with Legs in which you are weak does not mean relinquishing control. At the end of *every day* you need to draw up a quick mental balance sheet, asking yourself whether you have given each Leg enough of your time. If you have spent the entire day meeting with clients and customers, make sure you set aside enough time the following day to deal with your staff concerns, going over the actual merchandise or service operation with them. Don't ignore your accounts for more than a week, and make regular meetings with your book-keeper or accountant. The point is that even after you have 'outsourced' certain tasks, the buck still stops with you – you need to keep measuring the Legs to

*'Hiring experts does not mean
relinquishing control.'*

ensure that they are of equal strength and thus well balanced. Because without balance your business will eventually fall down like a house of cards.

CHAPTER 5

The Courage of Conviction – A Capital Plan

Raising Money

PRINCIPLE #8

'Building a business requires 90% guts and 10% capital.'

I have made the point already, but it is worth restating here: do not go to the expense of opening your own business before you've spent a number of years learning at someone else's.

Most successful entrepreneurs are people who launch businesses in the fields they were previously employed in. Without question, the twelve years I spent working for the Greatermans Group gave me not only the tools I needed to build Pick 'n Pay, but also the *clout* to persuade others to back me. Again, there are exceptions to every rule, and this is not meant to deflate the young entrepreneur with a brilliant plan and a headstrong attitude, but personal experience in a related field will stand you in good stead, not least when it comes to persuading someone to give you their money.

It is pretty self-evident that someone with experience in a relevant field, armed with a clear objective – one that embraces the principle of service, backed with passionate interest and sound research – stands a very high chance of success. Why then do so many people stay on the treadmill, caged in jobs they hate, complaining about how little money they make? What stops them from getting off and carving their own path? I've heard a lot of people say they can't af-

'Instead of allowing fear to paralyse you, or cloud your thinking, befriend it.'

ford to take the chance, but is it really about a lack of money, or just fear of failure?

Not that fear of failure is in itself a bad thing. I have already admitted that my fear of failure verges on the pathological. I worry about *everything*. But instead of allowing fear to paralyse you, or to cloud your thinking, *befriend* it.

Fear simply means you have the good sense to identify the potential pitfalls that lie ahead. By working with it – using the Problem–Cause–Solution and '7 Tried & True' analysis – you will be better prepared for any eventuality. But analysing consequences and calculating risk will only get you so far. At some stage you have to take the leap and follow your gut instinct. Just *do it*, even if it *seems* impossible. It will produce a kind of adrenaline rush that cannot be quantified. You may even find it addictive.

Note that fear is not the same as negative thinking, which you must guard against vigilantly. Do not heed doomsayers, such as the friend who cautioned me against starting my own business. 'Now is not the time,' he said. According to him, the 'best times' were over, that 'there was so much more opportunity during your father's era'. Unlike fear, you can do nothing constructive with negative attitudes, so brush them off (I deal with this in more detail in Chapter 17).

Of course, finding the right business and premises – one that sparks that intangible *'this is it'* excitement – helps to ward off negative thoughts. The minute I walked into the four little stores that the owner, Jack Goldin, had called Pick 'n Pay, I felt this terrific surge of confidence. The only problem was the asking price – at R620 000, the stores were way beyond my means. Jack Goldin had made it very clear that his asking price was not negotiable, so I accepted it almost immediately (along with a kick on the shins from my brother-in-law, who knew the price was way beyond what I could afford), and we shook hands. I had three days to raise the money, and absolutely no idea how I was going to do it.

I have been told that it was easy for me because I had a proven track record. It's true that I had spent the previous decade launching Checkers stores for the Greatermans Group, but not all of them had been a success. I had enjoyed the cushioning of a retail giant that had interests beyond food. More importantly, I had just been fired – and rather publicly so. Speculation was rife in all the business newspapers as to the reasons, which even I did not know or understand. So my reputation was, at the time, somewhat tarnished. But I believed passionately in what I wanted to do.

Having drawn up a balance sheet with every asset I could muster, I needed more money than any bank would be prepared to loan me. Then, as now, my first instinct was to reduce to an absolute minimum any reliance on a bank. A business loaded with debt, particularly to banks, is very, very vulnerable. Bankers can let you down. Interest alone can cripple you. Even if you have an excellent business plan and passionate self-belief, today's centralised process of approval means you have little personal contact with the person who will decide your fate. There is a good chance that he or she will say 'no' – certainly not the kind of demoralising assistance you should be courting at this early stage.

A 'capital plan' is needed.

Today, there are a number of funding options available to the entrepreneur. There are organisations devoted to finding and assisting fledgling enterprises with equity funding, either by becoming an investor or finding one to buy into your company. This is usually for a limited period, after which you have to purchase their interest in your company at the market rate. All banks are also now obliged by the Financial Sector Charter to aid and invest a percentage of their income in small enterprises. So, despite claims about an economic downturn and the like, there is always cash available to those with a simple, thought-through business plan, relevant experience and projected figures that are market-related and sustainable. These private-sector sources are discussed in the Appendix to this book, as are the kinds of government grants, subsidies and other incentives that currently exist in an attempt to kindle entrepreneurial growth.

In 1967, my options were comparatively limited.

I could have looked for a partner. This is a logical solution to limited funds, assuming you find someone who perfectly complements your skills, and is able to share the risks and capital outlay. Banks looking 'empirically' at a loan request will also favour partnerships between complementary persons 'of good repute'. However, I personally think taking on a partner is potentially even more dangerous than taking on a huge loan.

You have to be *very* careful about the kind of person with

'Fear is not the same as negative thinking. Do not heed doomsayers, such as the friend who cautioned me against starting my own business.'

whom you commit to co-own a business, as this is a legally binding relationship, with all the messy consequences of a divorce should it not work out. If you do fall out, the legal claims can absolutely ruin a business. That's not to say having a partner is definitely a bad idea – there are a myriad examples of successful partnerships. If you trust the person implicitly, go ahead. Just be aware of the consequences should things go wrong, and have a tight contract to cover both of your interests.

The other option was to look for investors or shareholders, rather than a partner or partners. For me, there was no contest. Investors are (ideally!) people who provide you with capital and expect you to grow their money but do not tell you how to do it (what is also referred to as a 'silent partner'). I knew exactly what I had to do; all I needed was the money to make a start, so this was the solution for me.

Most people think they don't know any investors, but you'd be surprised what you can uncover if you apply yourself. Aside from the private-sector opportunities referred to in the Appendix, please do consider presenting your business plan to a selection of family and friends. You have nothing to lose, and the best thing about these kinds of investors is that, given the element of trust that already exists, you can

'Taking on a partner is potentially dangerous. If you fall out, the legal claims can absolutely ruin a business.'

work to create structured loans that are not too onerous to pay back, thereby freeing you to really make *all* your money grow.

I could not have started Pick 'n Pay without the assistance of fifty individual investors whom my brother-in-law, my accountant, a good friend and I managed to gather together in the three days I had to raise Goldin's money. Their start-up investment capital helped persuade the bank to provide the rest. The structure of the loan and investment were also integral to the long-term success of Pick 'n Pay, which shows the importance of hiring the services of an astute lawyer and accountant at an early stage.

In my case, the proposal was structured so that half the investment was to be an interest-free loan for a fixed period of two years, meaning that each investor would be paid back 50% of the initial investment, with no additional money, after two years (remarkably generous terms, and to this day I thank my original investors for their confidence and vision). The remaining 50% was purely a capital investment, but we persuaded the investors to agree on a two-year 'window' in which I could build the business by ploughing profits back into the stores rather than paying out dividends. This meant that I gave away a very big portion of the business upfront in exchange for the capital to purchase it, but retained –

very importantly – the controlling interest, and without being crippled by interest or dividend repayments. What the investors gained were shares that rendered little in the very short term (two years is a blip!) but in the long term became very, very valuable. They gave me the space to build the business into a powerhouse in a relatively short space of time, and to rebuff a sustained and vicious price war with the Greatermans Group.

Why did they trust me with these incredibly favourable loan conditions? It's true that a few of the investors were friends or old school acquaintances, but most of them were relative strangers, connected via various friends of friends. We simply cast our net as wide as possible, calling on *everyone* to find *anyone* who was interested in backing my new business proposition. None of them were fools, nor were they necessarily of charitable disposition. They were not doing me a favour by giving me their money. They invested in my proposal because they believed it would deliver a profit. I am not sure if any of them foresaw quite how rich it would make them, but the risk was calculated. The point is that *I* was convinced, and my conviction was contagious – the outcome could only ever equal profit.

Essentially, regardless of *how* you raise the money – partner, banker, investor, equity manager, friend, family member – what you will have to do is *impress* them. Once you have won the commitment of a few, confidence tends to snowball, as nothing impresses one person more than evidence of cash investment from others. Everyone is swayed by other people's opinions, and whether it's a banker or 'angel

'If you believe in you, others are likely to follow suit.'

investor' (as an affluent investor who provides capital for a business start-up is sometimes called) the principle is the same: if someone believes in you, others are likely to follow suit.

But first, *you* have to believe in you. This is the fuel that will fire your courage.

CHAPTER 6

Research – Finding the Right Business in the Ideal Premises

Where to Open Your Doors

PRINCIPLE #9

'Better to overpay for a profitable business than fall for a so-called bargain.'

If deciding which business to pursue is bit like choosing a marriage partner, finding the right business or premises is not dissimilar to hunting for your first home.

Location, particularly for a retail outlet, is critical. If you get it right, you're made; get it wrong and you're sunk before you've even started.

Working through the '7 Tried & True', you would have decided 'where', ideally, you want to operate your business. It could be an area that you believe is underserviced (or 'understocked'), or it could be an area or city or region you feel a strong affinity for, or one that you are familiar with. Whatever the reason, having decided *where* you want to buy or launch your business, try to stick to this original plan; do not be distracted or deflected by possibilities that may arise in areas outside those you have identified, unless it arouses that strong sense of being just 'right'.

Always aim as high as you can afford. *Never* be tempted to settle on a bargain *just* because it is a bargain – unless the premises is solely a manufacturing outlet (in which case proximity to suppliers and distribution channels is still key). There are far more important considerations than price, including:

'Finding the right business or premises is not dissimilar to hunting for your first home. Location is key.'

Is it on the 'right' side of the street? It is vital that you know whom it is you are targeting. If your market is middle class, then you'd best open up in a part of town that is perceived as desirable. If your target market is more the bargain-hunter type, who may feel intimidated by a high-end environment, the 'right' side of the street may be what the aspirational shopper would describe as the 'wrong' side! If your market is bohemian and artsy, you need to choose a street or area that already attracts this kind of clientele. If your market never sees your business premises, you can locate it in an industrial area where rentals are far cheaper, and so on.

How visible will you be? Again, this is essential. Is it on a good thoroughfare, with enough passing traffic? When does most of the traffic pass? Is the passing traffic pedestrian or vehicular? Pedestrian traffic is ideal, which is why so many malls are so successful, but a busy main street may suit you and your business just as well. If the traffic is predominantly vehicular, this can either work in your favour (for a drive-through franchise, for instance, or if there is plenty of parking) or be a negative (a busy intersection is not usually conducive to the ambience of a fine-dining restaurant).

How adequate is the parking? The number of bays required will depend on your specific business needs but sufficient parking is absolutely essential.

Who are your neighbours? You will be associated with your surrounds, so a nearby Adult World outlet, for instance, would not be suitable if you were looking to open a childcare agency. If it is a new mall, are the anchor tenants big-name brands that will pull in custom? It may be worth your while contacting anchor tenants to find out why they are investing in the particular site, or to try and find out more about the size and kind of market they are servicing in a particular mall.

How near is the competition? It would appear to be common sense not to open up directly opposite or next to a competitor, but in fact competitive businesses that are complementary in some way feed additional customers to each other: in every instance where a Woolworths has opened where we were already an anchor tenant (and vice versa), *both* our turnovers have risen. Restaurants always perform better when they open up in close

'There is no merit in settling for something second-rate just because it is affordable.'

proximity to each other – as long as they offer different cuisines. But there is obviously no point in opening next to a competitor with whom you share parity of goods or services.

In addition to asking the right questions, you will have a gut feel for the premises that is right for you – again, not dissimilar to purchasing a home. If it doesn't exert a pull, don't do it.

Before I walked into Jack Goldin's stores, I visited a little chain called Standard Provision. On paper it was a pretty good deal, not least because it fell within my price range – around R150 000 – but, on inspection, Standard Provision just didn't appeal. It was a general merchandise store; I was a grocer and I wanted a supermarket. Maybe I could have made them work, but they simply didn't inspire me. The point is, I didn't believe – and still don't – that there is any merit in settling for something second-rate just because it is affordable. I went out on a limb to buy Pick 'n Pay, and never looked back. However, when it comes to premises (rather than a business), I must add that I have also walked away from a number of deals I thought very promising because I knew the business could not afford them. Always do the maths before signing a property lease.

PRINCIPLE #10

'Buy a business where the tea's already made.' – Ivan Lazarus

I was told this by a good friend when he heard I was looking to start my own business. It was, and is, very sound advice.

Just as renovating a house is usually more cost-effective than building a new one – assuming the foundations and existing structure are solid – so building a brand-new outlet or business from scratch is usually more expensive than buying an existing one, 'where the tea is already made'.

Building a brand-new business means you have to wait longer before you can start earning revenue, and if you're spending *borrowed* money at the same time ... well, that's stressful. By contrast, buying an operating business means you have immediate return on your investment as you don't have to build your customer base from nothing. With access to cash flow, you can start to service your debt and work on improving operations from day one. Having studied the books (and it is a good idea to bring in an accountant at this early stage), it is relatively easy to verify the profitability of an existing business, and this makes future income and expense projections much easier.

That's not to say purchasing an existing business is without risk. Study the assets and liabilities very carefully; a business that is just keeping its head above water but has many

> *'The best businesses are usually not advertised – more often than not it's being in the right place at the right time. But sometimes you can create that luck.'*

debts is easily crippled by a rise in interest rates. Physically inspect the assets – old, dirty equipment may need to be replaced, yet will be listed as an asset for which you will be paying. If the business is running at a loss you need to know why – is it because it is in the wrong area, or just poorly managed? Is it worth trying to turn around the fortunes of an ailing business by rebranding and relaunching, if the result is a loss in your initial customer base, for which you are presumably paying? Make sure you invest in a loss-maker *only* if you can clearly see where the problem is, and how to fix it, and that the cost of this is reflected in the price.

PRINCIPLE #11

'Keep your feet on the ground and your head in the clouds.'

Regardless of whether you opt to buy and revitalise a business 'where the tea is already made' or build one up from scratch, you need to match your dream business/premises with the reality of what's on offer.

Bearing your dream firmly in mind, you will now need to do the legwork, researching what's available and realistic in terms of affordability. Having defined your chosen trading area, get to know who's dealing in it. Speak to every agent, read the local papers, call the auction houses and explore the area by car and on foot. Get to know as much as you can about it – where the commerce nodes are, the schools and other places where the community gathers.

The best businesses are usually not advertised in the classifieds – they are snapped up as soon as word gets out, and more often than not it's a case of being in the right place at the right time. Luck certainly played a large part in how I found my business. But sometimes you can create that luck.

Jack Goldin might never have called me to offer his Cape Town stores if I hadn't taken the time to show him around my Checkers operation a few years before. I did so despite the fact that he was a competitor, because I don't believe in hoarding knowledge (see Chapter 14). I had spent an entire afternoon with Goldin, personally showing him how I ran my operation, and he returned to Cape Town to rearrange his operation in a similar way. And so, when I flew down to Cape Town to inspect Goldin's stores, it was as if these four small outlets were waiting just for me. Here was a supermarket chain run exactly along my lines. I didn't have to think about it. I knew I would do whatever it took to get them, and that I could make them even more profitable.

I discuss how I raised the cash in Chapter 5; the point is

that this business touched my heart, and my head. Similarly, your intuition will tell you when to make an offer, be it for a business or premises.

There are other ways of 'creating' luck. You need to tackle your geographic research with enthusiasm, following the initial legwork in a specific area with an analysis of current statistics and commerce trends (more on this in the Appendix). If you pursue this research with the same thoroughness as you have tackled the '7 Tried & True', I have no doubt that you will find a business or premises that is right for you. Remain sanguine as you attempt to match your dream with reality; if your first attempts fail, something better usually awaits.

PRINCIPLE #12

'Feed the bank, and you'll starve your business.'

I am often asked about the relative merits of renting versus owning the property in which you conduct your business.

Let's be clear: if you can afford it, you should be your own landlord.

However, most of us starting out in a new business are cash-hungry, and any money made must be ploughed back to service the business, not the property mortgage. Certainly

I could never have built Pick 'n Pay if I had purchased the buildings they were in at the same time.

So, as an overriding principle, start off by finding a property to rent, and redistribute your profits among the Four Legs of the Table.

Having decided to rent, you have to accept that you are going to have to survive what is for many people one of life's least pleasant relationships: dealing with a landlord. In the following chapter we will look at how best to negotiate and manage this relationship, so that the landlord's natural avarice and aversion to risk does not negatively affect your business interests.

As you get more successful, and the business more stable, it will be time to look at purchasing your own property. Be sure that the property you are interested in has business rights; if these are pending, make sure – in writing – that the sale is conditional to these rights. This may sound obvious, but I have made this rather expensive mistake and learned to stipulate in every offer to purchase that the deal is subject to the property being granted business rights.

Assuming your business keeps growing, as do your cash reserves, it is sometimes worth securing prime property you don't want, or can't expand into just yet – if only to keep it from falling into the hands of your competitors. You can then develop it to suit your needs, earning an income, and only utilise it for your own business later, at a highly affordable rental. But be careful: never allow the excitement of dabbling in property to distract you from your core business – unless, of course, that business is property!

CHAPTER 7

Negotiating – The Art of Persuasion

Getting What You Want

PRINCIPLE #13

'To win, you must be prepared to lose something.'

Being a tough negotiator is a pretty useful tool in *any* successful entrepreneur's arsenal, but it was – and is – the lifeblood of Pick 'n Pay. Not that I negotiated for the sake of it: every single discount was a saving I passed on to my customers. As such, I brought a keen appreciation and passion to the art of negotiating.

Before you enter the fray, you need to be mentally well prepared.

Negotiation is a game of poker, a battle of wits in which you have to bluff your opponent into placing all his cards on the table. He has something you want; you have something he wants. The trick is *never* letting on what your ultimate trump card is (usually, the price you are prepared to pay) before you have seen his or hers.

In order to achieve this, the first rule is that you must be prepared to lose the battle, or at least appear so, or you will never call your opponent's bluff. If you are too anxious to win, you will be at a disadvantage from the outset; your opponent will sense your enthusiasm, and your fear of loss. He will recommit to the fight, bending your will to his. Most of the best deals I made were ones I haven't really minded losing out on. This meant I could play it as I felt it – with a cool head, rather than having to hide my enthusiasm. Even if you really want the deal, you have to prepare yourself to play it as if the loss will not be that acutely felt.

The next crucial component is, *know your opponent*. You must have a pretty good idea of what's economical for both you and the supplier, and decide in advance the price and advantage you want to press home – not just how low (or high) a price you want to negotiate, but also more intricate incentives, such as an additional discount after reaching a certain sales target. If you are unsure where the boundaries lie, don't show it. Confidence is crucial. I used to carry a little black book that I would take out and flip through, then study one page in particular. With a pained expression, I would

> *'If you are too anxious to win, you are at a disadvantage from the outset. Your opponent will sense your fear, and recommit to the fight.'*

say, 'I see here that you have offered Checkers another 1.5% discount. I know I'm a smaller company but I won't be forever ... you've *got* to do the same for me', and so on. There was no way for the supplier to know that I was looking at an entirely blank page!

If you *are* the supplier, you should arrive having already built the discount into your so-called 'final offer' price, knowing you are going to be negotiated down. Or be prepared to offer another, final discount, based on payment within a certain number of days. Also, look at negotiating with more than just price – for instance, how you can improve or differentiate your service, like the baker who says he cannot afford to reduce the price any further but is prepared to deliver baking-hot bread three times a day. It makes no economic sense to squeeze a business with the kind of service ethic that money can't buy.

There are other small but important ways to help maintain the upper hand. Your demeanour is terribly important. You do not have to wear expensive clothes when negotiating the purchase of a new business or premises, or the terms of a loan, or when dealing with a new supplier, but there is no excuse for turning up at the negotiating table looking shabby. Show the proper respect, even if you think it's old-fashioned – men who saunter into meetings with their hands in their pockets are sending the wrong subliminal message. It's the same with being late; punctuality is not only a sign of respect but also – and this is another useful trait, and relatively easy to cultivate – of being well organised. A sense of humour is the greatest leveller, so keep yours handy.

Having decided what you want, and – should you not achieve it – that you are willing to walk away, go into the meeting and battle like hell for as long as it takes.

And time is often exactly what it takes. One of my chicken suppliers would sigh and shake his head when I arrived, then phone his wife to say, 'Raymond's here, looks like I won't be home for supper'. And it's true: I used to lose all sense of time when I was deep into negotiating a deal. I could spend hours negotiating a few cents, sometimes till 9 or 10 o'clock

'A sense of humour is the greatest leveller, so keep yours handy.'

at night, literally 'out-sitting' the guy, until I got my way. All in good faith and humour, with no raised voices. It helps if you really get on with your opponent. That particular chicken supplier and I used to play at the same golf club, and I could always tell a lot from the way he strode across the green: if his bearing was tall and cocky I'd know the prices he was charging were too high; if he looked a little slumped, I'd make a mental note to lay off trying to negotiate his prices down!

I also realised that I almost always negotiated a better price when I went to my opponent's office, and I did this no matter how big my company became. It doesn't matter if it's to negotiate a big property deal or a small shipment of merchandise, it's a courtesy to be the one who comes over. The subtext is clear – I am not the big guy here. It also means that the opponent is the host, and psychologically slightly on the back foot as a result.

Much as I enjoy the art of negotiation, there are two people I *never* negotiate with: my lawyer and my accountant. Find out who the best is – easy enough if you follow the word-of-mouth trail – and hire them. I knew I would pay through the nose, but I was happy to do so. The advice of the best law and accounting firms is likely to save you a great deal more money in the long run. Just get the best, and pay their price.

PRINCIPLE #14

'Don't give up until the deal is done.'

Unlike suppliers, property guys are usually more intransigent when it comes to negotiating. But the same techniques work – showing respect by going to their office, or taking them out to lunch, and not giving up just because they complain that you're being too difficult and prepared to pay far too little.

Don't give up just because enough time has passed, but know when to back off. I once almost lost a deal when a property developer, irritated by how late it was, called off the deal. I immediately took off the pressure, became as charming as I could, and asked if I could take him to breakfast to make up for it. Which is where we finally settled (and yes, on the rental I wanted). It's amazing how persuasive real passion can be; if you can make your prospective landlord believe in your business and your acumen, thereby assuring his rental, and have some fun in the process, half the battle is won.

Whatever you agree to with your prospective landlord, make sure it is in writing and signed off by the right parties. Unlike merchandising, where a handshake can signify a done deal, a property deal is only binding if it's in writing. We took a lot of risks with property in the early days, buying merchandise for a store while still negotiating the terms, sometimes to our great cost, until we started insisting on signing at least a Heads of Agreement document (listed in the Appendix).

When it comes to negotiating the rental figure, you will need to know what the going rate is per square metre in that particular area, and work out if you can afford it. I had to guess what turnover was when negotiating with landlords for new sites; rental had to be 1 to 2% of turnover, given how slim gross margins were. If the site is good (which is why you want it), you're unlikely to get it for much less; in fact, the landlord is likely to try and sell it at a higher price per metre. Again, remember that it is worth overpaying – if you can afford it – rather than going for a bargain *just* because it is a bargain.

I do not like inflation clauses or fixed annual increases! We tend to negotiate a fixed rental figure for the first five years – in other words, no annual increases in the first five years, then a 3 to 5% increase for the next five years, and so on. But there is no cast-iron rule in property; you will simply have to negotiate as hard as you can, then give in graciously.

The confidence you have in your business and the premises will no doubt determine the length of your lease, but you should in most cases try to negotiate for the longest lease possible; with a short-term lease, an opportunistic landlord will invariably raise the rental substantially during the next round of negotiations, knowing that you will be loath to move your operation. Twenty years may feel like forever, but from where I am sitting it's over very quickly. We tended to negotiate twenty-year leases with at least two five-year options. This means you have the option to renew your lease for effectively another ten years; today I wish we'd negotiated four five-year options!

'Try to negotiate for the longest lease possible. Twenty years may feel like forever, but from where I am sitting it's over very quickly.'

A last point on negotiating with landlords (or their brokers): given that you are entering into a legally binding contract, do not be rushed into signing, even if you are told that there is 'another interested party' who is (as you will be told without fail) 'ready to sign' – you need time to do due diligence on the space, cost what you will need to do to make the space ready for custom and study the lease carefully. Be wary of signing what the landlord may describe as his 'standard lease'. Remember that the interests of the landlord often stand in direct contrast to yours. To ensure that you are not laden with hidden or unnecessary costs, and that the lease is structured to protect your business interests and not just those of the landlord, I'd highly recommend you consider hiring the services of an expert to examine and, if necessary, amend the contract before you sign. Lawyers are useful in this regard, but it may serve your interests even better to contact a company that specialises in lease negotiations, as they truly understand the consequences of what is often hidden in the fine print.

Regardless of the kind of contract you'll be signing, I'd recommend you make sure that the following two aspects are included:

1. That you are allowed to *sublet* to another business during the lease period (so long as the business is legal, or any

small understandable and non-limiting clauses the land-lord may wish to add here). This will limit your damage should you have chosen the wrong site or the business fails.

2. That you leave the property at the end of the lease with *wear and tear accepted.* This is crucial, as it protects you from any unreasonable demands the owner may make in terms of returning the property in the exact state he or she rented it to you regardless of the improvements you may have made.

CHAPTER 8

Empathy & Empowerment – The Guardians of Your Greatest Asset

Finding – and Keeping – Great Staff

PRINCIPLE #15

'Belonging is even more important than believing.'

For practical reasons, people may not be entered as assets onto a company's balance sheet, but this does not mean they shouldn't be viewed as such. Regardless of how good your ideas, how sophisticated the equipment or how great the premises, a business is only as good as its people. Your mission statement means nothing unless your employees make it come alive. Your premises will stand empty without their warm welcome; your equipment will be ill used without trained personnel. These facts are obvious, but how to find – and keep – the best people possible remains for many an elusive Holy Grail. People are the second most complex Leg (after Administration) to grow and maintain, as the many books written on the subject attest. For most entrepreneurs, it is also the most costly – salaries usually represent 50% (or more) of your expenses.

If you want a real return on your investment, never knowingly underpay an employee. But, as I have said before, no one works *just* for a salary. No matter what the money, no one wants to be part of a cold, unfeeling machine.

I am always saddened when I hear of entrepreneurs who see their employees as a major headache, and actively work to reduce their number. Staff relations may be complex, but

'If you want a real return on your investment, never knowingly underpay an employee.'

a business that is hampered by capacity is like a pot-bound plant – struggling to thrive. It is only when you find the right people, and are able to inspire them to commit what is, after all, the greater waking part of their day, that you will see the best possible return on your investment.

We all know that employees need to feel safe, secure and comfortable to perform at their best. If you have a temper, do your utmost to restrain it. Challenge employees with training programmes or educational opportunities to develop latent talents (but make sure they are contractually obliged to reward the company for the investment). Most importantly, make sure each and every one understands the importance of his or her role in the company, along with the boundaries of acceptable conduct, and the consequences of neglecting either. But to turn an average worker into a good worker, and a good worker into someone truly brilliant, takes something less tangible. No matter how small the concern, you need to make the people who work for you feel part of it, that they *belong* to something.

I tried to run what became a very big business along lines similar to when it was small. Central to this was recognising that I was never above the interests and concerns of the people who worked with me to build the company.

Loyalty, like respect, cannot be bought, only earned. You

earn it by showing a real interest in your employees beyond the confines of what they can do for your business – individual expectations and hopes, achievements and losses must be observed and, if possible, acted upon. Don't *talk* about how much you care; show it through your actions. This is leading with integrity.

You're not expected to become a counsellor or friend, but an employee who is going through a truly tough time – a divorce, losing a parent, or coping with a seriously ill child – will never forget the tacit support they receive during this difficult period, and will reward you with renewed vigour and long-term loyalty on their recovery. If a senior employee becomes terminally ill, make every effort to go and see them. It may appear expedient, but the gesture will mean the world – not only to the person and his or her family but to the remaining employees of your company. In the unfortunate event that someone in the company dies, make every effort to find time to go to the funeral. You may think you can't spare it, but this is what old-timers call 'doing the right thing', and doing the right thing not only feels good, but the wave of appreciation and gratitude evoked by such an essentially small gesture far outweighs the time saved by not doing it. Most people don't like funerals (understandably), and employers may find all the reasons in the world not to go ('it is a private affair', 'I hardly knew the family', 'nothing to be gained', 'too many meetings', and so on). Cancel these thoughts along with your plans, and go. Aside from anything else, it is an essential pause in the maelstrom of life.

PRINCIPLE #16

'Get your hands dirty.'

There is little that inspires employees more than seeing their leader working, really working, alongside them. Of course, this is far easier in a small company, when your presence is virtually guaranteed on the shop floor (or whatever your particular 'coalface' is!). But as the company grows, so do the demands on your time. It's then that you will find yourself increasingly office-bound. Leaders who get tied up in meetings, delegating, travelling, administrating and overseeing tend to lose sight of how much their physical presence can motivate employees. Make every effort to stay connected by spending time with them, even if it is only to shake hands and inquire after the quality of their week-end, along with more pertinent work-related queries. Just do it – being seen and heard by 'the boss' has inestimable value. Include everyone – even those employees who are considered the least important. Your interest and acknowledgement can mean the world to someone used to being treated as fairly invisible. It shows, concretely, that you are not above the concerns of your employees' lives, despite the growth of the company, and that you remain accessible to even the so-called lowest members in your company hierarchy.

When a company grows too big for you to have a personal handle on individual employees, develop an internal human resources (HR) department, with a professional at the helm, to deal with employee recruitment, motivation and discipline. However, don't let this lull you into a false sense of security: you still need to spend time with the guys on the floor – leading by example, and demanding the same from your senior managers. Up to the day of my retirement, I insisted on personally greeting every new employee at head office, remembered many staff members' birthdays and tried to participate in as many of our company events as possible. Knowing how much this has meant to Pick 'n Pay staff, I intend to continue playing this role well into my twilight years.

> *'Leaders tend to lose sight of how much their physical presence can motivate employees.'*

Not every entrepreneur is by nature a 'people person'; many find it difficult to empathise with staff concerns when there is so much else at stake. If this is you, hire someone in an HR capacity sooner rather than later. Remember that there are also other, less 'touchy-feely' ways of showing appreciation and inspiring loyalty in valued employees. Having said that no one goes the extra mile for a salary alone, this does not mean that money is unimportant; it stands to reason that if you pay the top salaries in your particular industry you'll have the best people lining up to work for you. I was horrified recently when I was told by a business colleague that we had to guard against 'salary creep' as 'times were tough'.

He reasoned that we couldn't go on giving salary increases 'indefinitely'. No salary increases? If times are that tough, you will have to consider closing shop.

Aside from a good salary and a clear job description, everyone needs something to aspire to.

People love titles. I admit I am guilty of exploiting this. Giving a title is an easy (and cost-effective) way to recognise and reward an employee for achieving excellent performance levels, or to inspire others to reach for and maintain high performance levels, thereby creating an aspiring trend. Where titles become problematic is when they start to create hierarchy. Having too many levels in an organisation can be demoralising, even stressful, to employees who find themselves further and further away from the power base (more about my passion for flat organisational structures in Chapter 13). Titles do not *have* to denote hierarchy; they can often simply recognise exceptional performance. Even in a small organisation you can reward and inspire staff by instituting an Employee of the Month award, or Go the Extra Mile badge, or Best Green Initiative, and so on (I deal with harnessing our competitive natures in a little more detail in Chapter 12).

These are all good ways to reward key staff, but for those staff members whom you feel are truly invaluable to the smooth running of your business, I believe there is nothing quite as binding as an employee shareholding scheme.

PRINCIPLE #17

'We make a living by what we get, but we make a life by what we give.'
– Winston Churchill

It stands to reason that making an employee effectively a co-owner is the most powerful incentive there is, demonstrating both your commitment to the individual while simultaneously locking in their commitment to the company.

Over and above salaries, I have over the years given away millions to my staff in the form of shares, and it hasn't made me poorer. Quite the opposite. Being generous to your employees comes back in the way they care for your products *and* your customers. This 'psychic ownership' in turn reduces shrinkage and generates increased revenue – yet another form of enlightened self-interest, which I deal with in more detail in Chapter 15.

It is of course much easier to put into place an employee shareholder scheme in a public company, where auditors have determined the capital value of the company and decided on the number of shares before the market decides the shifting value of every share, but a similar process can be followed for a private company. Auditors will value your company and provide an independent, unbiased figure of its worth. Taking this into account, you can devise a legally binding yet informal shareholding scheme by issuing what is known as 'ghost' shares. You will need an accountant to assist, but bear in mind when working with ghost shares that the highest number of shares at the lowest rate will give you more flexibility for employee shareholding schemes; for example, if the capital invested in the company is R500 000, it is better to issue 500 000 shares at R1 than 50 000 shares at R10.

Be cautious about who you hand shares out to – equally so the valuation process and the terms under which an employee can cash them in. Make sure that the share is linked not only to a performance target but also to a clearly stipulated period of service (around five years; longer is onerous), and that the agreement is null and void should the employee be fired, join a competitor or emigrate. As owner, you must also have first option to purchase the share. Share numbers being finite, you will, to maintain an employee shareholder scheme, have to constantly buy shares as they come on the market, so that you can continue to give them away while still protecting your controlling interest.

Initially, I made the mistake of giving away far too many shares to too many people. In my eagerness to reward as many staff members as possible, with no clear guidelines, it was distressing to find that some, as a result of a misguided sense of overnight riches, got themselves deeply into debt, while others undervalued their shares and immediately sold them. As time passed, I became more circumspect about who I gave shares to, and as a result I have managed to retain key members of staff who would otherwise have left to start their own companies or enriched my competitors' coffers. Giving away shares has since become more complicated thanks to new taxation laws aimed at employers and employees who have used shares to avoid paying tax (for example, paying a below-par salary with the balance made up in shares, which used not to be taxed), but I still believe in the power of share options to not only motivate but empower people, and I continued to give them away right up to my retirement.

PRINCIPLE #18

'Employ empathy.'

Do not sully your reputation, or your sense of worth, by doing the wrong thing by your employees. Ill-treating someone who works for you has serious consequences, not least those of a legal nature. Not that I am suggesting you do the 'right thing' simply because you don't want to upset the labour unions or end up in court. There is a deeper principle at work here. Aside from creating a happy workforce, doing the 'right thing' is good for the long-term reputation of your organisation, as every person who comes into contact with your business becomes part of your PR, and that includes your employees. This has never been more true than today, with the power of social networking via the Internet elevating everyone to the level of reviewer and critic. But even more important than these 'self-enlightenment' considerations is the humility you need to hold onto when building a business – with all due respect, can you really do it on your own?

Mostly I have tried to do the 'right thing' by my employees because I always knew that without them I was just a one-man-band grocer selling goods on the side of the street. I really appreciated what they gave me, and wanted to *show* my appreciation. I did this by never forgetting how I would have liked to be treated when I was an employee. Naturally I was hurt on the occasions when my appreciation was felt as somehow lacking. Like all relationships, the employee–employer one is complex, and there is no foolproof, one-size-fits-all philosophy to make it work. But here, for good measure, are some guidelines to hiring, promoting, outsourcing, retrenching and firing that I picked up while finding my way.

Hiring

I built Pick 'n Pay with people who other companies may have bypassed; at least, I don't know many employers who, from the very outset, looked for the attributes I did.

Certainly, I am not one for brilliant A-grade results, or graduates from fine establishments with proven track records. The right *attitude* is more important to me than qualifications or work experience. You can train people in various skills, but you cannot change their character. Aside from anything else, attitude and character are often evident in body language; someone who slouches, for instance, is unlikely to be a quick thinker or to show much initiative.

I am a firm believer in the benefits of *practical learning*: spending formative years in the right working environment

'The right attitude is more important than qualifications or work experience. You can train people in various skills, but you cannot change their character.'

can achieve more than an Oxbridge or Ivy League (or any other exalted) education, which can create an inflated sense of self-worth. I preferred, when possible, to hire young school leavers, matriculants who were exhilarated by their new-found independence and the possibilities of life, and then to train and promote them as and when their experience and skills warranted it.

I also tended to look for people who have been active across a broad spectrum of things, not just doggedly pursuing academic excellence or sporting achievements. Well-rounded people tend to be more *adaptable*, which means you can move them should the initial appointment not suit.

Enthusiasm is of course key: with real enthusiasm you can never go too far wrong. Even if the person turns out to be less than ideal for the position you've hired them, an enthusiastic employee will find a valuable place elsewhere within the organisation.

I have an equal penchant for *kindness*. This is perhaps the most undervalued of the characteristics I have learned to cherish over the years. Being kind doesn't mean being soft. It's simply acting as humanely as possible in any given situation. I value it as highly as enthusiasm, and not purely for altruistic reasons. Kind people will permeate an organisation

'Kindness is perhaps the most undervalued of the characteristics I have come to cherish. I value it as highly as enthusiasm, and not purely for altruistic reasons.'

with a caring attitude; not only will this result in an atmosphere in which employees are helpful and supportive towards each other, but it will spill over to the customer experience.

Aside from considerations around character, you are well advised to be familiar with the current thinking on employment equity, not only in terms of diversity but also disability, and to get up to speed on your regional employment equity requirements. (You will find more guidance on this in the Appendix.)

Lastly, it is worth doing things by the book from the outset: providing your new employee with a clear written contract in which his or her job description is stated, as well as the terms of dismissal (making sure there's a clearly defined trial period during which you will not be penalised should the relationship not materialise), wages, leave, disciplinary procedures, and so on.

Promoting

It's old-fashioned, I know, but I am in principle averse to head-hunting and a firm believer in skills training in order to promote from within: I would honestly match any of my GMs, all of whom have come up through the ranks, most of them with no university degree, against any MBA-graduated CEO in South Africa.

No matter how expert, outsiders take time to train – in everything from understanding the operational logistics to the vague but equally important values that define the culture of an organisation. They can cause bitterness and sour relations among your own rank and file. Aside from this, an individual who has worked their way up through the ranks has real insight into the kinds of problems and concerns that people have at every job level, and this helps to create a multi-skilled staff with a flexible approach to job descriptions. So, not only does promoting from within provide your existing employees with a sense of stability, hope and fairness but there is minimal wastage of human resources.

In recent years, I have been persuaded by advisers to 'enhance the gene pool' by bringing in outsiders. While I still fundamentally believe in promoting from within, the skills injection has proved useful in some areas. But, for the most part, the graduates from our 'good made great' apprenticeships have always outstripped the imports.

Outsourcing

There are those who believe in outsourcing as much as possible. I'm wary of this approach. You can outsource so much that you're no longer running a business! Of course, there is no point in doing something in-house if an outside specialist can do it better, or just as well but more cost-effectively. As your business grows, you will come under increasing pressure to hire outside specialists rather than expand in-house departments. However, you do need to look at more than just the bottom line here.

As a general rule, I recommend that *no department or function fundamental to the strength of the Four Legs ever be outsourced.* Given the complexity of the fourth Leg (People), human resources is a vital component, and any failings are very costly indeed. You have to have the courage to look after your people, no matter how big you become. This is virtually impossible if you hand over control to an outside company, which will invariably focus on maximising resources, often at the expense of the individual's faith and sense of belonging.

Retrenching

I have never been very good at dealing with what is rather insensitively called 'dead wood' – especially, of course, people whom I have worked with for many years. It is true that some people peak organisationally when they are young, particularly in industries where youthful inspiration or looks are prized, but I think it is iniquitous to fire an employee in their fifties, having squeezed their best years out of them.

You can't keep someone on for sentimental reasons, but generally speaking it is better to re-utilise someone than to get rid of them, even if it costs you more in the short term. I don't believe in retrenching, but rather in atrophy; I have done the maths, and in a large organisation it will often cost you less – financially and emotionally – to bide your time and wait for people to leave than to pay out the sums required to get them to go.

If you have purchased a new business and inherited its workforce, remember that you are dealing with a highly skittish and demotivated team, one you will no doubt have dif-

'In a large organisation it will often cost you less – financially and emotionally – to wait for people to leave than to pay out the sums required to get them to go.'

ficulty turning around. Ignore your entirely understandable instinct to make a clean sweep and turf them out like old fittings. Treat these inherited members with the humanity and humility you wish your company to be associated with, looking after them as if you had hired them yourself. Either they will rise to the challenge or, again, a natural process of attrition will take place.

Firing

It is a thoroughly unpleasant experience to dismiss an employee, but as the owner you should have the courage to do it yourself, particularly if you were the one to hire him or her in the first place. It's not something any of us relish, and it is never easy – not least because you will have to follow diligently and consistently the procedures you have set up on recruitment. As such, firing someone is very much a last resort.

If there is one misdemeanour that makes the process easy for me, it is dishonesty in general and theft in particular. *Never tolerate dishonesty.* If you suspect someone, don't be a patsy: act immediately and confront the culprit. Occasionally, we use lie detectors to try and identify or corner a suspect, but this is by no means a foolproof method and, if inconclusive, can destroy the trust and cohesion within an entire department. But in essence, if you have evidence or strong suspicions, the process is pretty straightforward: 1) confront the culprit; 2) tell him or her that if, *and only if*, they tell you the truth you won't involve the police, but that if they keep denying it you will have no choice but to let the law take its course; 3) get rid of the person the minute they confess. If there is no confession forthcoming, you will have to offer some kind of severance, and if this is not accepted you will need to involve an expert in labour law to facilitate the tedious process by which you extricate yourself from your contractual obligations.

'Be tough, but, most of all, be generous.'

There are other, less obvious, forms of dishonesty than theft. Poor accountability is one. Power can go to people's heads. Taking on the title of 'manager' does not turn anyone into a big shot with a sense of entitlement; this attitude is the antithesis of co-operation and can result in poor management decisions based on ego rather than objective weighing of factors. Equally distressing is the process by which blame is shifted where it doesn't belong, often in an unconscious attempt to save face. Employees willing to take responsibility for mistakes, without excuses, do not deserve your ire.

Whatever the reason, once you have decided to get rid of someone, do not beat around the bush. Having called the person to your office, do it quickly; often, they are expecting it.

If it is a mistaken appointment rather than a serious misdemeanour, do not have a basket of platitudes ready: the only real way to minimise the disappointment is by being honest, and exceedingly generous – work out how *much* you can pay, not how little. It may be a result of my own experience – being called in on a Monday and told that I had to clear my desk that very morning, and dismissed with no more than two weeks' pay – but I take umbrage at the prevailing attitude of 'how can we get rid of this guy as cheaply as possible?' Be tough, but most of all be generous. I usually have a gut feel as to what is fair (you can and should also take advice from a lawyer) and I go beyond the legally required figure. Aside from it being the right thing to do, it is not worth getting bogged down in court cases and having your energy sapped by issues and persons that should no longer have anything to do with your business.

CHAPTER 9

Pricing – A Tricky Business

Putting a Value on Your Product or Service

PRINCIPLE #19

'Never confuse turnover with profit.'

Pricing is a very tricky business.

It's a question that comes up time and again: how do you *know* what prices to charge? Well, you don't really! A lot of it is guesswork. Start by knowing what your competitors charge. Then make an educated guess at your projected turnover (as this will affect volumes, and therefore purchase price due to discounts etc), look carefully at all your expenses, and determine what percentage these will be of your projected sales. Remember that turnover is no indicator of profit; for that, you need to estimate your margin – the difference between the purchase price you paid for an item (or what it costs to produce) and the price at which you sell it.

The size of your margin depends on the business you are in. Some businesses deal strongly in perceptions rather than real value – diamonds are just shiny baubles, but most of us are quite happy to pay a relatively large amount of money for them thanks to a clever long-term marketing strategy that has elevated them into highly desirable, sought-after and expensive items. Other items are extremely labour-intensive, such as a tailor-made suit, or hand-crafted wine. A jeweller or fashion designer making bespoke pieces would of course approach pricing very differently, looking to make 200% or more on cost; here, price is less important than the perceived, emotively charged value of their time. In this kind of industry I have met entrepreneurs who have actually sold more *after* they put their prices *up*!

The luxury goods market aside, most industries are striving for a competitive edge by providing the same service or product at a lower price. Some even choose to enter the market by selling below cost. Be careful of this strategy; any fool can sell below cost, but it's a dangerous business. If a competitor starts carving into your market share with this strategy, keep a cool head. You can't ignore competition that hits you hard, but you also can't respond in such a way that you end up broke. If a competitor offers an item at a vastly reduced price, either try to meet his price by negotiating with your supplier to get a better deal or strike back with ten other desirable items at greatly reduced prices. But a deep, sustained price war will kill you both.

Food is a basic item, and as a food retailer I wanted to embrace the principle espoused by Bernard Trujillo of providing my customers with a widely accessible choice of mass-produced goods at the lowest affordable prices. The rule was – and is – simple: overall, margins of profit per line simply have to be as slim as possible. Most customers are very sensitive to hikes in prices, so with a tiny margin there is very little leeway when you are faced with unexpected expenses. Better therefore to balance the comfort of a higher margin (as long as you can still remain competitive) with your responsibility to provide your consumer with a fair price.

When working on all of these factors – turnover, expenses,

margins – make sure you are working in *percentages*. Many people erroneously assume that when an item purchased or produced for, say, R100 (having fought like hell to get the cost there!) is sold for R150, they have made 50% on the cost. It's a terribly dangerous assumption because by measuring the difference in currency terms, you are not actually measuring the *percentage*, which is the *only* measure you need to take into account. The R50 'made' on that item represents an increase of 33.3% – i.e. you have made 33.3% on the purchase price, not 50%. So if your expenses are 35% of your sales, you're running at a 1.7% loss, a mistake that would be compounded if you mistakenly believed you were making a 50% profit, thinking that you have a nicely padded gross margin of some 15%. This is a surprisingly common mistake, and one you must vigilantly guard against, bearing in mind the dictum that 'profits are not optional', as the Chicago entrepreneur Jay Goltz once blithely said.

PRINCIPLE #20

'Create islands of loss in a sea of profit.' – Bernard Trujillo

Regardless of where you pitch your product or service, an experienced merchant knows that you have to entice your

'There is always wastage somewhere in the business; the trick is to keep looking for it.'

customer in some way, or, as Bernard Trujillo put it in his typically pithy way: 'You need to create islands of loss, in a sea of profit.' The 'island' is a deeply discounted loss-making line (or service) used to reel the customer in, knowing that she or he will spend more on other, higher-margin items, thereby creating your sea of profit. Take the example of a small café in a shopping mall serving a premium coffee at the same price competitors are charging for a cheaper brand. The café will pull in more customers, knowing that the 'loss' will be made up by the sandwich or breakfast most customers will order to accompany the coffee that tempted them to sit there in the first place. Every business should have an 'island of loss' – preferably one that no one else has – that is balanced by higher gross-margin items.

At one stage, the expenses in my bakeries were 40 to 50% of sales, while my gross margin was only 25 to 30%, which meant that I was losing money hand over fist in this department. Was the entire bakery an 'island of loss'? I went over to the US just to study their bakeries, and learned that even within departments you can, and should, create 'islands of loss'. According to this principle, basic loaves of bread can be priced with loss-making margins, but your top-end speciality breads can carry far higher margins; the customers who put these in their baskets have a lower (or no) barrier to higher prices, so therefore they help carry the cost of cheap bread for the man-in-the-street. It's a case of constantly measuring and adjusting all items – if you see that customers purchasing luxury items don't notice the higher margins, you can adjust them upwards a fraction and adjust your island of loss downwards, to the benefit of the highly price-sensitive consumer. This measurement and balancing needs to be made monthly, looking at turnover and expenses (both as percentages) of loss-making lines and how they are carried by those higher-priced items. If you don't keep measuring, you go broke.

PRINCIPLE #21

'It is better to have 50% of something than 100% of nothing.'

Do not be greedy. It is tempting to maximise profit on a desirable item or service, but opt rather for fair pricing. Large margins may produce a quick profit, but this more often than not encourages a relaxed attitude to expenses – something you may only realise once there is a downturn, by which time it is too late to recoup those losses. Small margins force you to control your expenses vigilantly. And of course small margins mean you're price-competitive, which invariably means increased custom, which results in potentially far larger profits, as your turnover keeps apace of your growing reputation for good value.

Integral, then, to managing cash flow (dealt with in the

next chapter) is controlling expenses. There is *always* wastage somewhere in the business; the trick is to keep watching out for it, and to implement the necessary changes before expenses erode your margins. This is yet another reason why you will probably need help with the Administration Leg; with someone recording up-to-the-minute expenses, you can tell at a glance where you are. Another pair of eyes to pick up and alert you to sudden swings and trends, not to mention help with looking at ways of reducing wastage or managing increases, will soon outweigh the cost of hiring a good book-keeper or accountant.

'You cannot expect your staff to respect the boundaries of ownership if you plunder the business at will.'

The wastage that hurts the most – if you let it – is 'shrinkage': loss due to theft or damage. No matter how vigilant you are, thieves – sometimes customers but, sadly, more often than not your employees – will find ever-more-inventive ways of augmenting what you already provide. As such, shrinkage is a non-negotiable part of your business expenses and one you need to budget for from the outset. Different businesses will allow for different percentages; at Pick 'n Pay we aim for zero shrinkage by offsetting gains made elsewhere, but even with this flexibility we never achieve zero shrinkage. The best way to deal with shrinkage is – like all expenses – to watch it like a hawk and, at regular intervals, compare figures and determine how close to zero you are. When you see a surge in loss in a particular line or area of the business, you have a practised thief in your midst. Call in the police, put your own detective skills to use, install CCTV cameras, employ a lie detector – whatever it takes to catch him or her, or them. Don't be disheartened or take 'shrinkage' as a personal affront – it occurs in absolutely every business. Lastly, lead by example: you cannot expect your staff to respect the boundaries of ownership if you plunder the business at will, as dealt with in the next chapter.

CHAPTER 10

Self-discipline – Managing Cash Flow

Running a Tight Administrative Ship

PRINCIPLE #22

'No one ever went broke through having too much cash.' – Donny Gordon

It's simple: no cash, no business.

If you pay your suppliers too early and invoice your customers too late, you will go broke. If you expand too quickly on borrowed money, you will go broke. If you don't watch your expenses like a hawk, you will go broke. Get the cash in, control your expenses and stay liquid – keep investing in the business but not at the expense of cash reserves. It's no use investing in more equipment or staff if there's not enough money available in the bank to make the monthly commitment. And if you're a public company, think twice before paying dividends if the result is weakened reserves: access to cash is paramount. Only once you have built up your cash reserves can you operate from a position of strength – able to consider paying dividends, looking after your employees better than your competitors, investing in new equipment, implementing new accounting systems or updating your technology, whatever is most essential to maintaining or growing your share of the market at the time.

Healthy cash flow comes from running a tight administrative ship – the first Leg, and from a personal point of view the most frustrating and difficult one to maintain. Here, then, are a number of ways to ensure that you build one that is strong enough to support the business.

For the starter entrepreneur, it's vital to plan an achievable cash flow scenario. First and foremost, that means coming up with a realistic estimate of your expenses, your projected turnover and consequent income. Be conservative (but not over-conservative) with your sales estimates. You need to research this scenario very thoroughly, and plan the timing for the various payments you will need to make, and when you can realistically expect income (assuming it's not a COD business).

Leave nothing out when working out your estimated outlays. If at all possible, avoid leasing anything other than your property. Leasing is just another form of debt, and you know by now that I believe debt is generally to be avoided like the plague. Leasing also reduces profits on your balance sheet due to the over-cautious new accounting system, International Financial Reporting Standards (IFRS), which requires that all leases are entered using an annual average, which is not a real cost but an artificial figure. Profits are motivating for all the stakeholders in a business, so I don't believe in artificially reducing them.

There are numerous expenses in any business; the following list is by no means comprehensive but you will certainly need to include estimates for:

- salaries (usually the largest expense in any business, in excess of 50% of your total expenses)

- merchandise/stock

- rental/rates

- loan repayments

- shrinkage

- insurance

- electricity

- communication/computers

- banking

- equipment/fixtures

- stationery

- PR marketing

- transport

When you are working on your what/where/why/when/which/how/who, it is also worth planning for an emergency contingency cash fund to cover unexpected eventualities, ensuring you have enough cash to stay afloat even when unexpected disaster strikes. These can be as varied as a prolonged strike or terrorist attack, a poison scare or recession – anything unforeseen but possible, and not covered by insurance. The amount needed will depend on your business and your particular set of expenses. A lot depends on the terms you have agreed with your suppliers, as well as the agreement

'Negotiate the largest possible overdraft figure with your bank. Once the business is doing well, renegotiate.'

you have with your bank, but the usual rule of thumb is to have enough money in reserve to cover your expenses for at least three months.

Aside from setting aside a healthy percentage of profit for this reserve, negotiate the largest possible overdraft figure with your bank. Once you have been in business for a few years, and the business is doing well, renegotiate for the most favourable terms you can; the bank is more likely to provide you with generous terms to remain liquid at that stage than at the start of your enterprise. Increase the overdraft to a figure as big as the bank is willing to agree to. Although I don't like to borrow, you simply *must* have this back-up in place in case there is an emergency, as well as to cover you during those inevitable times when income slows while payments accelerate. An overdraft is another expense, of course, even when not in use, so make sure this is budgeted for as well. As important as this overdraft is, do not let it lull you into a false sense of security. Nothing must replace your drive to grow healthy cash reserves – this is the only real security, and will protect you from borrowing at extortionate rates or, worse, from being refused or foreclosed.

As discussed in Chapter 4, the first, most important step towards managing your cash flow successfully is an honest self-assessment. If your strength does not lie in the administration of the business, hire someone. Finding an account-ant isn't difficult; you could find one through the Chamber of Commerce, or, given that accountants can become quite specialist, you could call an organisation representing your business interest, or call a few of your competitors and ask them for the name of their accountants. You may not need a qualified accountant for the day-to-day running of the administrative Leg. I'd advise against hiring someone with no experience. You'll be looking for someone who is a stick-ler for detail, someone with office management skills, who knows something about structuring wage packages, tax re-turns and other statutory requirements. This is not some-thing you can put off 'until you've made enough money' to warrant it – if you have no experience or interest in office management, hire someone to do this, even if part-time, and make sure it is done properly from day one. If you are really convinced that your business is so small that it does not require outside help and you think you are the kind of person who can manage the minutiae of administration, give yourself a trial period of two months – if you are not tallying expenses and sales slips once a week, then you do not have control of your business. Don't berate yourself, or make excuses. No one but you is listening. Just accept that you need help, and get it.

I recently advised a young man who had identified the need for better waste control, and had come up with a bril-liant plan – a timeous response to the poor recycling sup-port given to consumers with a green conscience. He was dynamic and passionate about his business, but was struggling to keep his head above water. When I looked at the business, it was immediately apparent that his administrative Leg was wobbly. When I pointed out how essential it was to manage this effectively, he said he understood but couldn't afford to hire an additional person. I persuaded him that this was not a saving, that in fact he couldn't afford *not* to hire someone, and that his business would finally topple if he didn't. He went home and discussed it with his wife, and discovered that his mother-in-law had some accounting experience. He was able to hire her on a flexible trial basis to help ensure that invoicing was done on time and followed up regularly, that expenses didn't pile up, that there was less wastage and generally better control of cash flow. Within a few months, the benefits in terms of improved cash flow were so apparent that he was considering expanding his operation nationally. (Incidentally, I advised against expanding so quickly, not wanting him to run before he could walk. But he chose to ignore me, and now has a very successful national operation – proof that sometimes advice is, and should remain, just that!)

Again, hiring someone to run the administration of your business efficiently is not an invitation to hand over entirely to some other 'expert' – quite the contrary. You have hired someone to do the nitty-gritty business of chasing income, paying expenses and recording cash flow, but in the final analysis you are the one who makes, pays and manages the money, and adjusts business practices accordingly. You need to study the books, going through the expenses and sales with a fine-toothed comb, looking at ways to increase

'How you choose to invest your own income is an entirely personal affair, but never put the company at risk.'

the cash flowing in while reducing the cash flowing out. Note that while it is not in your interests to pay suppliers as quickly as they would like, it is better to pay faster than your competitors are prepared to, either extracting a discount in the process or simply with the aim of developing a good long-term relationship.

Assuming you are succeeding in this exercise, you will soon have enough set aside to cover expenses for three months; now you need to think about where to put the surplus profits. As the availability of cash remains crucial, don't invest your cash in any lengthy, long-term projects; the maximum time period you should have to wait before you have access to it should be around thirty days. Never chase interest rates. I have always viewed those that promise an exceptional interest rate, particularly for a prolonged period of time, with caution if not downright distrust; the likes of Bernard Madoff have ensured that I am no longer alone in this view. Given these caveats, the best place to ask for advice about where to place surplus profits is probably your bank rather than a financial adviser who may be more interested in risk, and whose advice is likely to cost more. How you choose to invest your own income is an entirely personal affair, but never put the company at risk.

PRINCIPLE #23

'Never treat your business as a personal piggy bank.'

As important as never confusing turnover with profit is the discipline to budget a decent salary for yourself, and then stick to it.

It is a fundamental mistake most start-up entrepreneurs make. Pay yourself a predetermined salary from the outset. No one can live on nothing, so if you have not budgeted an adequate salary the business will starve you, or – the more inevitable course – you will help yourself to what's in the cash register. But cash is turnover, not profit. Many entrepreneurs, starry-eyed at the sight of cash flowing in, will rush out to buy themselves matching BMWs, with only a vague sense of the actual expenses that go into their business. Some even rationalise that it is the owner's right, after all the stress and strain of getting the business off the ground and keeping it afloat! In a couple of months they're broke, wondering what happened.

The business should never be a vehicle to fund your lifestyle, but a healthy entity able to pay you a salary, no matter how meagre, with profits ploughed back into the business. You have to exercise enormous self-discipline, particularly if it is a cash-rich business, because the temptations are very real to see this as your personal honeypot. But it's the kiss of death for anyone with a long-term view to building a strong business. Even if you do manage to keep paying your expenses, a business that shows no profit is not worth anything to anyone. And forget about ever having it accurately valued for resale purposes.

> *'There's nothing worse than watching the owners siphon off the profits. Say to yourself: "I am an expense", and budget for your salary.'*

Aside from this, it is thoroughly demotivating for employees. Whether you are working for a large or a small business, there's nothing worse than watching the owners siphon off the profits. Say to yourself: '*I am an expense*', and budget for your salary; it may be minimal or it could be above the going market rate, but it must be included along with the budgeted salaries for your employees in your expenses. If there isn't enough money to pay yourself a salary, you need to cut expenses elsewhere. 'Self-employed' means that you are employed and therefore entitled to a salary. What you are not entitled to is to treat your business like your personal piggy bank. Your business is a third party, separate from you, and the profits belong to the business. If you do not run a tight, honest ship, making a clear profit and paying the relevant taxes, you cannot expect to interest anyone in investing further.

CHAPTER 11

Serving Your Customer – Three Cast-iron Rules

Growing Customers

PRINCIPLE #24

'Treat the customer like a queen and she will make you king.'
– Professor William H Hutt

It was during the third 'Modern Merchandising Methods' seminar I attended in McAllen, Texas, that the slightly disgruntled Harrods representative put his hand up. The seminars, held every quarter during the 1950s, had fast become legendary. Up to a thousand delegates from around the world, including the big retail names like Sainsbury's, Marks & Spencer, Carrefour and now Harrods, came here to learn from the retail genius, Bernard Trujillo. Trujillo wasn't a retailer himself, but he was deeply passionate about modern retail methods and their ongoing evolution, spending weeks travelling around the US to identify what was working, and where, before sharing his latest philosophies in the simplest, most charismatic way.

Trujillo had just made a slightly salacious point: that modern retailing methods had to be a lot like Marilyn Monroe – 'desirable goods, openly displayed and readily accessible' – raising several eyebrows, as well as the hand of the Harrods delegate.

'I'm very sorry, Mr Trujillo,' the man said, standing up. 'I do not think that the Queen, whom Harrods serves By Appointment, can be expected to shop in this kind of environment.'

Bernard didn't miss a beat.

'Tell me, buddy, how many queens do you have?'

There was a ripple of laughter, a release of tension. Those of us who had attended a few earlier seminars knew that the idea that any one customer should enjoy precedence over another was anathema to Trujillo. The customer, every customer, came first. When another dissenter had questioned whether they would still be able to make money if they slashed their margins and asked customers to weigh their own food and push their own trolleys, Trujillo had dug into his pockets and pulled out a fistful of cash. 'Money? This is not about money!' He threw it at us, notes fluttering down. 'You're not in the business to make money! You're in the business to serve your customer and fight on her behalf for the lowest prices. Fight for her, and she'll bring you your profit.'

Trujillo was quite a showman. I don't think anyone who was there that day forgot his point – treat the customer as a queen, fight for her as your sovereign, and she will reward you with her custom and her loyalty.

Central to treating your customer as a queen is courtesy. You will turn every stranger who interacts with you and your employees into a loyal customer if you treat him or her with the kind of courtesy you would instinctively give an important guest in your own home. And note: everyone is a potential customer – be it your suppliers, accountant, consultant or a visiting salesman. Make sure that every level the visitor encounters, from your security guard to your receptionist or secretary, is staffed by courteous and welcoming people. And never keep anybody waiting.

Similarly, you need to treat every potential customer with

*'You will turn every stranger into a loyal
customer if you treat him or her with the
kind of courtesy you would instinctively give
an important guest in your own home.'*

kindness. Show people you care by remembering things about
them – from the simple, like a name, to the more demanding, such as their personal preferences. It's what successful
old-fashioned restaurateurs have known for years: a sure-fire
way to keep 'regulars' coming back is to greet them effusively
by name, ask them if they would like to be seated at the same
table, whether they will be needing the usual bottle of wine,
and so on. Yet the tricks of the hospitality trade are so seldom
deployed in other businesses.

Of equal import is to show gratitude for their custom. Not
lip service (such as a prerecorded message or printed till slip)
but a real, sincere 'thank you'. These days, there's a lot of
fuss made about loyalty schemes – cards, usually working on
a points system. While these certainly work, and in a sense
reward the customer by giving something back, it is a very
conditional way of saying 'thank you'. You don't have to be
a genius to work out that the real function is not so much
'thank you' as 'keep spending your money here'. I believe that
it is far better to say 'thank you' by supporting local community charities and fundraisers (discussed in more detail in
Chapter 15). People also love getting something for nothing –
a biscotti with their coffee, an upgrade, a bouquet of flow-
ers, a free sample bottle, a balloon for the kids, the Sunday

newspaper. Loyalty schemes only recognise and reward regular followers, but if you try to find a way to reward all your customers with something unexpected and pleasant, you will end up with more regulars.

Assuming you are offering a price-competitive product or service, your business is efficiently managed (clean premises/functioning, well-maintained equipment/helpful, efficient staff) and you treat every customer with courtesy, kindness and gratitude, you cannot fail to grow.

PRINCIPLE #25

'Be humane.'

Being humane – observing your customers with empathy – may gain you more custom (and cost far less!) than a fancy ad agency.

Watch, listen, and *use* your innate insight. Why is there a rather dejected and dishevelled woman frowning at the shelves in the baby section? She is clearly a new mother, exhausted and somehow frustrated by the choice. I witnessed a Pick 'n Pay manager in just such a situation approach the woman, asking if he could help. She shrugged and said she was desperately looking for her baby's specific milk formula, but it appeared we didn't stock it. The manager took her details and had it delivered to her home the very same day, and ensured that the shelf space for the product was made available during the week. That woman will never forget the insight, kindness and responsiveness of that store manager. Similarly so, a woman looking forlornly at the bread baskets; she was doing a big Italian lunch for friends, she told the baker, but there was no ciabatta ready. The baker arranged to have it delivered to her home as soon as it came out the oven. Or the customer who wanted to make a vegetable stew and wanted a specific mixed bag – a staff member arranged to have it delivered to her home from another branch. Or the new deli counter lady who made up an entertainment platter to a customer's exact specifications, despite the fact that she had never done anything like it before. I was, and remain, inordinately proud of these Pick 'n Pay staff members, as I am of the many, many, many more, whose genuine commitment to customers makes our mission statement come alive.

Aside from observing and responding to your customers *in situ*, do the research. Pick a few random customers and try to find out what it is they like, don't like or feel is missing from your business and its products/service/atmosphere/ experience. Customer satisfaction forms are a common way to gauge where improvement needs to happen, but many customers see these as impersonal ('Does anybody actually read these?' is a common refrain), not to mention an imposition on everyone's increasingly limited time. Staff are also an invaluable source of information – some managers let their employees pick the product lines to put on promotion, often with exceptional results.

'The old-fashioned methods – getting to know your customers, and giving them not only what they need but surprising them with your intuition and care – still apply.'

Try and be creative about your research into what 'desirable goods' your queens need by identifying niche markets. These are wonderful because they are cohesive homogeneous groups, defined by nationality, religion, age, socio-economic background, school, Facebook following or general indicated preference for just about anything you can think of. If you have an online business, you can follow your customer's 'purchase trail' with ease, and even predict what she or he may like based on items already purchased (such as Amazon's suggestion that you may like the following books based on the one you just ordered). In time, marketing will become so personalised that every purchase decision you make will make it easier for similar products to be targeted at you (something I am not sure we should be looking forward to!).

But the old-fashioned methods – getting to know your customers, and giving them not only what they need but surprising them with your understanding and care – still apply. It's been years since my wife Wendy and I went to see all the embassies to find out what food items their employees (and, by extension, any first-generation foreign national living in South Africa) really missed, and went out of our way to give them a taste of home, but we still try to identify and satisfy needs. Sometimes all it takes is to look at existing markets with new eyes; in the new Pick 'n Pay franchise stores in Limpopo, traditional items such as whole chicken feet, hearts and mopani worms are not only 'openly displayed and readily accessible' but beautifully laid out in trays under glass counters in the deli section, showing the same respect for the local queens' delicacies as Parma ham in Hyde Park or Gorgonzola cheese in the V&A Waterfront.

PRINCIPLE #26

'Connect your employees to your customers.'

Whether it is understanding or pre-empting your customers' needs, or simply providing a royal service, your employees' attitude is crucial to the customer experience. You can invest in market research, or customer surveys and carelines, but you'll need a pretty large operation to warrant the spend. Inspiring your employees to serve and learn about customer needs with the same passion you do is both more subtle and effective.

Employees tend to emulate their leaders. If they see you genuinely putting the consumer first, treating each and every one with courtesy and kindness, there is a good chance they will too, particularly if you have hired people who display these characteristics naturally. Often, employees simply don't grasp their connection to the customer's experience, and how the customer in turn sustains their salary. Work tirelessly to make this connection crystal clear.

Equally important (and, for many, much more challenging) is to treat your employees the same way you wish them to treat your customers. The way staff treat customers is often a direct reflection of the way management treat their staff, so make sure that the characteristics you wish your customers to experience – courtesy, kindness and gratitude – are part and parcel of the atmosphere at work.

Last but not least, look at regular incentive programmes designed around customers nominating and complimenting staff members who go out of their way to make the customer experience memorable. This is a way to both encourage and recognise staff members who go that extra mile, and again reinforces a direct connection between customers and employees.

PRINCIPLE #27

'Complaints can make a business.'

Even if it's not in your nature to welcome criticism (and heaven knows it's not in mine!), you must remain totally receptive and respond in a supportive, apologetic way. Subsume your personal ego to your business persona; you will win more

'You will win more friends by successfully handling a complaint than by spending a fortune advertising your wares in the press.'

friends by successfully handling a complaint than by spending a fortune advertising your wares in the press. A strong, positive response to a complaint says that you understand the courage it has taken to speak up, that you take seriously whatever the customer has complained about and that you are ready to rectify the situation. This is how you can turn virtually every criticism into a PR opportunity, and transform the most upset customer into a friend.

I know it's a cliché, but the customer is *always* right, even when he or she is wrong. Unless it is a reprehensible attack against an employee, such as a racially based insult, this is a non-negotiable rule. It is, for instance, why Pick 'n Pay has always accepted returns without question. For the one or two who behave fraudulently, there is a legion with legitimate complaints, and we would all do well to listen to the few who bother to speak up.

Should you find this policy abused by a complainant who keeps coming back to criticise, you will soon pick up the pattern, but initially you simply have to accept the customer's complaint as legitimate, and respond with good grace. If you struggle with this concept, see it as a self-enhancing exercise in control and a way to grow personal power. In this way you can transform your ego's instinctive defend-and-attack position into a far more useful ally, one that understands there is more to be gained in the long term by turning a potential enemy into a powerful ally than simply winning a small but damaging battle. Because you haven't lost just one customer during a badly handled complaint – one customer's badmouthing can lose you at least ten more.

We all know what it's like to be served a below-par meal: it takes a certain amount of energy to report this to the waiter or manager. If the response is a snooty 'no one else has ever complained', you will not only never return, you will actively persuade others to do the same. If the response is a luke-warm apology, you are unlikely to return, or will react with hesitation at any later suggestion to go there. If, however, the response is profusely apologetic, and some compensation is offered, it is likely to make up for the bad meal. In some instances, it can leave you feeling even more positively inclined than had you had an average meal – because the management showed it cared.

'It will cost you far less in the long run to be generous and subservient than to be high-handed and dismissive.'

Some complaints are more serious than others. A customer who slips and falls and claims that you are liable is dangerous. Always try to restrain tempers. Try not to get lawyers involved. Our lawyers have instructed us that, should someone fall in our stores, we are not to assist as this may be admitting liability. Nonsense! I don't care about liability when it comes to courtesy. We do what we believe is right, and that is to show the customer that we see her as our queen. However, we are grateful for the advent of CCTV: a customer who hobbles in with a plaster cast ready to sue for negligence will be silenced when you replay the footage of her in the store the day before, showing clearly how she stumbled, fell and then walked off without difficulty. Like so many seemingly unaffordable expenses, it will in the long run save you more than it cost to install.

Whatever it takes, do your very best never to end up in court over a customer dispute, as – regardless of the outcome – the process may damage your reputation beyond repair. It will cost you far less in the long run to be generous and subservient than to be high-handed and dismissive.

CHAPTER 12

Competition – Within and Without

Harnessing a Driving Force

PRINCIPLE #28

'The ability to learn is the ultimate competitive advantage.' – Jack Welch

I don't think I had ever looked forward to a game of golf as much as this one. It had taken months to find a date and place that suited both of us, and yet here I was, calling Ernie Els to cancel. One part of me was kicking myself but the other, stronger voice – the one ever on the lookout for new ways to look at my business – was telling me that I had to, that I was about to embark on something important.

I was in Europe for the annual CIES conference (CIES being the French acronym for the International Committee of Food Retail Chains), which had ended the day before. At the closing event I had struck up a conversation with Fritz Alquist, an old acquaintance and head of Albert Heijn, a very successful Dutch chain of supermarkets. Albert Heijn had just started franchising, and when we got to talking about the possibilities, Fritz had promptly invited me to accompany him to visit one of his first franchise operations the next day. The store was about 100km outside of Amsterdam, so here I was, driving through the flat Dutch landscape when I could have been walking the greens with Ernie.

'We were thinking of closing this store,' Fritz was explaining. 'The location wasn't that great and it needed substantial reinvestment. We weren't sure if it was worth it. As an alternative, we offered the store as a business to one of our managers. We said he could retain the name as long as he ran it with the same attention to detail he had run Albert Heijn for us. He didn't think twice. He just leapt at the chance.' Fritz shrugged. 'It's incredible. In the first two weeks the store had a record turnover. What had been an ailing store, a drain, has been turned into a success.'

When we met the manager-turned-franchisee, I could see why. The man was a live-wire, brimming with enthusiasm, despite the fact that he said it was the toughest thing he has ever had done in his life.

'I've been doing everything from scrubbing floors to stacking shelves; I've got my wife in the deli, and my daughter in the bakery. None of us has ever worked so hard in all our lives!'

'That's great,' Fritz said dryly, with only the hint of a joke, 'but why didn't you work like this for *us*?'

It was a crucial insight. By giving his manager the greatest level of control – his own business – he had devised a way to fan the strongest competitive fires possible. I've always encouraged what I call intrapreneurial behaviour (as discussed in Chapter 13) by giving as much freedom and independence as possible to each region and store, providing managers with their own budgets for every department. The corporate office threw a very light rope over their operation, providing guidance in terms of buying, promotions, advertising and finance, but essentially each region was free to do whatever they wished.

The concept of a family store being franchised to a manager entrenched in the ethos of the business made *so* much

'Never be scared to copy a good idea.'

sense; it meant we could turn around stores that were really floundering while keeping talented intrapreneurs in the family. On the one hand, we had a number of run-down stores that needed to be energised by the kind of indefinable extra that comes with running your own business; on the other, we also had a few top guys in their late forties and fifties who were getting itchy feet. Giving stores to our experienced black managers also fitted in with our commitment to real BEE transformation – not some shop-front decoration but real, independent ownership.

I took the concept home, feeling as excited as I did when I first walked into Goldin's four stores back in the 1960s. It was a perfect fit, one I immediately wanted to try out in Pick 'n Pay.

I had a hell of a battle with the board. It took me months to persuade them but eventually they relented, and gave me one store to try it out. As I predicted, it was a huge success. Today we have 332 franchise stores, of which 108 are entirely black-owned and managed – that's empowerment with a capital E.

Like so many of my initiatives, this was not an idea that came from some deep well of inspiration. I simply kept my eyes open, saw the idea, liked it and copied it. The lesson is simple: never be scared to copy a good idea. There is no copyright on knowledge, simply an ongoing process by which we keep improving on each other.

I once got a call from a gruff-voiced American saying he'd heard a lot about our hypermarkets, and would I be prepared to send him some plans and explain how they worked. The voice belonged to Sam Walton, founder of Wal-Mart. At that stage Wal-Mart had no food department, and Sam had heard that Pick 'n Pay was pretty well organised. Sam was a classic 'grasshopper economist', interested in everyone and anything, but I was still impressed that he chose to research his expansion by contacting a relatively insignificant grocer in Africa. I was even more impressed when I finally visited his superstores and realised they were a virtual carbon copy of our hypermarkets!

I believe that it is possible, with the right attitude, to learn something from just about everyone – a principle that is so important to me that I devote the next chapter to it. But I mention it here because nothing fans the competitive flame more than harvesting and studying the best ideas.

PRINCIPLE #29

'People play harder when there's someone to beat.'

I am a terrific believer in the power of honest competition in an open, free market. Nothing lights a bigger fire underfoot or makes you strive harder, and it produces results that far surpass what you envisaged.

When I started Pick 'n Pay, I didn't expect Checkers to react so aggressively – or so soon. I had only been in business for a year when the big chain I had created for Greatermans moved in for the kill, launching a sustained and vicious price war in the Cape that I could never have won. Their nationwide income meant their provincial bottom line could remain in the red while I slowly bled to death. But, as we all know, dig someone else a hole and you may very well be the one to fall into it.

I responded by expanding Pick 'n Pay nationally far sooner than I intended. Greatermans' aggressive attempt to cut me down in the Cape raised my competitive blood, and resulted in my business flourishing into a nationwide operation that grew bigger and healthier, faster.

I think most people are competitive by nature. What you have to do is work out how best to harness this natural instinct, considering whom you want to inspire, how to sustain interest and what you expect to achieve.

At school, I always played harder for a house match than I did against other schools, and I don't think I am unique in this respect. You only have to watch provincial supporters at a game between the Stormers, Sharks, Cheetahs or Bulls to see the truth of this! As your business grows, and you hire more people, you will often find that staff will act far more competitively *within* the business, competing *against each other*, than they will with outside competitors, despite the fact that the outside competition is, rationally, a far bigger threat to job security.

Within reason, this is a good thing, and, if well utilised,

'Competition must be managed. An aggressively competitive atmosphere can be divisive and contrary to the cardinal principle of co-operation within the company.'

can help to create a highly motivated staff, a more efficient division and, ultimately, a better-run business. Everyone needs something to aspire to. Usually it's a promotion. But with flat management structures, discussed in the next chapter, you do away with people simply coveting the position above them, opting instead to create pools of colleagues or divisions working competitively alongside each other. The prize? Recognition.

With the natural, even geographic, separation you have when different divisions or outlets compete against each other, it is far easier to ensure that competition is a unifying force rather than purely adversarial. But competition must be managed, particularly in a small operation, or it can have unforeseen consequences. Always carefully gauge the atmosphere and spirit in which the competition is carried out: an *aggressively* competitive atmosphere can be divisive and contrary to the cardinal principle of co-operation within the company.

To encourage people's naturally competitive nature, goals must be clear-cut and attainable. You don't want it to degenerate into an aggressive game in which staff are pitted against each other, producing 'winners' who lord it over demotivated 'losers'. There should be plenty of opportunity: hold varied competitions to recognise strengths throughout the company, and reward a variety of people – for example, Employee of the Month, Best Display, Most Caring Person or Best Green Initiative. The competition must be held in good faith and spirit, with plenty of effort spent on encouraging participation across the board. Essentially, it is the climate you create that will determine the atmosphere of the competition. People feel proud to work for a company whose objectives are essentially good, and when they feel proud of the company they tend to combine their ego-driven desire to come first with a more altruistic sense that the ultimate aim is to build a good, strong company together.

PRINCIPLE #30

'Listen to the whispers of tomorrow.'

I am avowedly anti-cartel, anti-monopoly, anti-collusion, anti anything that fixes prices. The idea of two or more competitors getting together and 'fixing' an outcome appals me. So too the industries in which there is only one supplier. But an honest fight in which the best man (or product) wins is thrilling, and results in the only fair outcome for the consumer.

But, as is so often the case with ironclad convictions held

in youth, the years have tempered my militant support for free trade. I have come to see that unfettered competition can be dangerous. While I think most governments tend to stick their noses where they shouldn't, we all know what happens on busy roads when the traffic lights break down – chaos, even carnage, ensues. I spent many years fighting various cartels, and relished breaking supplier stranglehold price-fixing, but I admit now that the old agricultural control boards also played a vital role in protecting farmers, who face a precarious life dependent on far too many factors beyond their control. This was evident in 1996, when the government introduced legislation to scrap the control boards, with the result that the price for maize shot through the roof. Despite the fact that enough maize is grown here to feed virtually the entire country, poor South Africans suddenly had to pay the same price as someone living in New York, or Siberia.

Clearly, then, competition without any sort of regulation can be immensely damaging, but the problem is where to draw the line: should government control competition, or should it be the job of collective business forums? Either way, some sort of control to protect the consumer from the vagaries of the weather and volatile international markets would be welcomed. While the 2009 Consumer Protection Act does neither, it is a welcome step in the right direction, assuming your company is truly there to serve your customers rather than simply chase profit.

CHAPTER 13

Building a Great Management Team

The Argument for Flat Organisational Structures

PRINCIPLE #31

'It's amazing what you can accomplish when it doesn't matter who gets the credit.' – Harry S Truman

Flat management structures are not fashionable. Call in most management consultants and the first thing they will do is recommend a chain of command. This makes things easier for managers – usually the ones who hired the consultants in the first place – but it is not necessarily good for business.

I experienced the inefficiencies and frustrations of hierarchy first-hand during my years as a manager for Greatermans. I have always thought of myself as a team player, but at Greatermans I developed a reputation as a difficult person because I could not see the point in giving in just because someone with grey hair said I should. My suggestions were constantly thwarted by senior management, who thought that the old way – their way – was still the best way to do things. The Machiavellian man at the top of the pyramid believed in splitting power to keep his staff compliant and his ego protected. I had no control over the buying or accounting departments – core to the bottom line I was expected to produce. But worse than the divide-and-rule principle, which left me rudderless, was the system within my own department, whereby I had to report to the

'By providing direct access to power, employees feel their ideas and passion are noticed, which inspires them to keep putting forward new ideas.'

man above, who reported to the man above him, and so on. The red tape I had to get through to present suggestions to the top meant that I could never be sure how my proposals were being presented, or why they were being turned down. It also meant I could never make a quick decision on anything. It crippled me, and was at the core of the failure of Checkers division to really take off in the early days. Having suffered in an environment that crushed innovative thinking under the heel of bureaucracy, I was determined to one day work in an environment where everyone had access to power, and therefore a sense of real control and accountability.

Of course I am not suggesting that a large company can survive with an entirely flat structure – this is unfeasible. Every company must have a leader. But I think there are enormous benefits for those leaders who try their darndest to reduce the levels below them.

Here are some of the benefits of flat structures:

1. **The positive psychological benefit to your employees is enormous.** By providing direct access to power, you empower the people working under you. They feel that their ideas and passion

are noticed, which inspires them to keep putting forward new ideas. Researchers monitoring the levels of stress hormones in chimpanzees have apparently found that these are reduced in those chimpanzees socially close to the alpha male, while those living at the bottom of the hierarchy, with little access to the leader or control over their lives, produce far higher levels of stress. We may be more complex primates, but my most stressful years were at Greatermans, when my attempts to talk to decision-makers were blocked at every turn.

2. Flat structures make for a more accountable workforce. Hierarchy, while efficient, implies that some are at the bottom of the pile, and blame tends to shift that way. The bigger your business, the more problematic this becomes. Flat structures suggest that everyone working in a business is essential to its success, making it more difficult to 'pass the buck'.

3. Flat structures allow for quick action on potential threats or opportunities. In *The Four Legs of the Table*, I compared the benefits of flat, decentralised structures to that of having a fleet of fast destroyers able to outmanoeuvre the huge battleship, with its unwieldy chain of command. With flat management structures you can anticipate an outside threat faster, and move quickly to neutralise it. If you have to go through two or more people in order to reach a decision, you will lose precious time (and with it, potential customers).

4. Flat structures allow you to accurately measure the emotional temperature and wellbeing within the company. It's not unlike a large extended family; if everyone, from the youngest to the oldest, feels that he or she can approach the patriarch at any time with his or her concerns or achievements, you will have a cohesive family unit. But make the eldest child the spokesperson for the rest of the children and before long you will have trouble in the family.

5. Flat structures create a meritocratic culture. If you have worked in a large organisation you have no doubt found yourself sidelined at some stage by someone pursuing his or her own 'empire-building' agenda. Such people usurp your efforts and present them to the person above them as their own. Everyone gets pushed down into 'pockets', and the portals of power are jealously guarded by the insecure and the ambitious. This is simply not possible in a flat organisational management.

The criticism of flat structures is twofold. Firstly, I have been told that hierarchy provides every aspiring employee with

*'If you have to go through two or more
people in order to reach a decision, you
will lose precious time (and with it,
potential customers).'*

a goal to work towards, and can therefore work as a strong motivational force. I have no truck with this. While I too believe strongly in the value of competition as a motivator (as discussed in Chapter 12), I am of the opinion that competition occurs as easily in flat structures as it does in a hierarchy.

Secondly, it is said that a leader who has too many people reporting to him or her will not have enough quality time to truly lead all of them. This is a reality, and you need to watch that you don't overburden yourself, or your managers. Management consultants tend to limit the number of people reporting to one person to five or six; personally I think a strong leader can have up to ten people reporting directly to them. After all, if you have hired the right people, having them report to you should not be so onerous. My advice is not to have the number circumscribed by anyone or anything other than your capacity. You'll know when it is too much; don't stop until it is.

Of course, the reality is that if you have pursued a management structure that works, the resultant growth in employees will finally make a flat organisational structure unwieldy. When this happens, you can simulate a flat structure by using a combination of direct and dotted lines on the organisational diagram. In a smaller organisation, the dotted line can simply indicate an open-door policy, in which you make it very clear that you will never be too busy for anyone who works for you (and then follow up on this promise!). But as your organisation continues to grow you will need to work in a more formal, structured way to keep everyone connected.

In addition to a direct line linking an employee to the manager they report to, we created a series of dotted lines linking every senior person to the top layer of the organisation, or, in our case, to the corporate office. In this way you had, for instance, all store managers reporting to the regional manager, and the regional managers reporting to the general managers who report to the CEO – all direct lines. But in addition to this you have a dotted line connecting the corporate head specialists, such as the head of Buying, or Social Development, or Advertising, with all the regional managers and store managers.

Essentially, the dotted line means that that there is access and information flowing both ways, with the person above performing an overall guiding role rather than the day-to-day interface of the direct line. If used regularly, the dotted line will help ease the burden of a leader with too many people reporting directly to him, yet it prevents the creation of rigid levels, with important people (as indeed almost everyone is) shoved way below the reach of their leader or managers sitting in an ivory tower. Leaders do not belong in ivory towers; they must be at the front line within sight, sound and touch of their followers.

PRINCIPLE #32

'Make your managers feel like kings in their own castles.'

The driving force in a growing business lies in harnessing the energy of what I call 'intrapreneurs'. This is an employee who thinks and acts like an entrepreneur – always questioning, always looking at ways of improving the business, always trying new things to add value – yet remains loyal to your company.

Often these people are seen as troublemakers – too honest, headstrong, difficult, unreasonable, always fighting the status quo. As they don't blend into the existing corporate comfort zone, they are often ostracised and made to feel unwelcome, and finally forced to 'migrate'. If you have an employee like this, don't make the same mistake: an intrapreneur is like gold, and must be treated as such.

Naturally, this includes a good remuneration package, but this alone is not enough to keep the intrapreneur's interest alive. Even more important to the intrapreneur than remuneration packages, and even shareholder certificates, are *space* and *control*. The intrapreneur needs room to experiment and an overall sense of being at the helm of his or her own ship: this is the only way to keep the intrapreneur's passion and interest focused.

This, then, is yet another reason why I am an ardent believer

> *'Highly centralised management makes employees feel that they are paid merely to "do", not to think. It kills the intrapreneurial sparkle.'*

in flat, decentralised structures: highly centralised management makes employees feel that they are paid merely to 'do', not to think. It kills the intrapreneurial sparkle. To keep intrapreneurs immersed in your business as if it were their own, you simply have to give them the freedom to feel as if they are, to a large extent, in control; that they are kings in their own castles. This is exactly what flat management structures achieve, encouraging the intrapreneur to take ownership of the business. In tandem with this freedom is a clearly defined limit to their authority – I always told my managers that they were free to do anything they wanted, as long as they did not lie, cheat, steal or buy Anglo American (at least, without my permission)! In the broadest sense, managers are then free to make their own business decisions without reporting to you, as long as every decision is preceded by the following three questions: *Will it be good for the business? Is it in accord with our values? Can we afford it?*

So, aside from any other consideration, flat management structures work for intrapreneurs. And without intrapreneurs to help grow the company, the size of your business will always be defined by one person's capacity: yours.

PRINCIPLE #33

'Always get both sides of the story.'

The first, most important rule in any conflict resolution is to listen to both parties, and never more so than when the conflict is within your management structure.

Listen to both sides of the story independently, without the other party being present. Listen empathically and objectively, without choosing sides. If you value both managers, it is irrelevant who, if any, is 'right' or 'wrong'; what you need to do is understand where the problem lies.

Once you have heard both sides, apply your analytical mind to solutions. Again, it doesn't matter who is right or wrong, or even what is fair or unfair – if both parties are highly competent and key to the business, you need to find a way to keep them both. Work through the problem from every angle, using the '7 Tried & True' (see an example of this at the end of Chapter 19). As it is unlikely that you can restructure your management team in such a way that the two parties will have no direct dealings with each other, it is time to bring the conflicting parties together and facilitate a compromise.

Try to do so in neutral territory, preferably away from work and home, so that they are free from the distractions of colleagues, family and friends. Lay down the ground rules: each party will have a turn to speak; neither party is to interrupt the other while speaking. Set the goal: that the desired outcome is not that one of them will 'win' the battle, but that both now have an opportunity to really listen and try to *understand* the other person's grievances, while simultaneously feeling heard and understood, and together find a solution that makes the most of the positive attributes each brings to the business. Human nature being what it is, this will probably mean working together on structures that separate duties and minimise contact.

If this intervention does not work, you will be forced to choose.

This is a terrible situation for an employer. But no matter how hard, you need to be decisive and act fast to root out the rancour, as it will seep into the atmosphere at work.

The normal rule of thumb is always to back the man (or woman) who outranks his or her 'opponent'. But before you take this step blindly, think carefully about the characters involved. Which one is more likely to guide the business according to your mission statement rather than his or her own ego? Which one do you trust to lead your people with empathy and kindness? You know which I would choose.

Having made your decision, be ruthless. Elsewhere I have stated that you create a culture of loyalty by backing and supporting your employees, even when they make mistakes. We all make mistakes, after all. However, if you know an employee is bad for business, he or she must go. Your first loyalty is to the company, which employs so many more.

CHAPTER 14

Humility – Never Know Enough

Not Being Bigheaded

PRINCIPLE #34

'Keep your ear so close to the ground the grasshoppers can jump in.'

There's not an original idea in this stupid head of mine! Nearly everything I am, or have done, I pinched, or else it 'grasshoppered' its way into my life.

This is because I never let my ego get in the way of a learning experience – or at least I try my darnedest not to!

It is true that some entrepreneurs are arrogant, and their cockiness can be inspiring to a certain sort. But it is difficult to be a good listener when your voice is the loudest, and impossible to learn anything if you think you know it all, or pretend you do. Humility enables you to listen and learn, while modesty lets you give others credit, which in turn forges the greatest, most long-lasting relationships with colleagues and clients.

A 'disease of entitlement' is rampant in South Africa. Arrogance, the belief that you are somehow superior to anyone else, that it is OK for others to have to wait on you or for you, or give way to you simply because you have more power or money or fame, goes against my whole being. Like kindness and courtesy, humility – especially when displayed by the powerful to the so-called ordinary person – is a very underrated characteristic.

Humility can have a bit of a Uriah Heep image – a kind

'It is difficult to be a good listener when your voice is the loudest, and impossible to learn anything if you think you know it all, or pretend you do.'

of creepy, ingratiating sycophancy. That's not the humility I am referring to, which is simply about not being bigheaded. No one gets ahead in life without some sort of help along the way. The trick is never to forget this. Remember that you were helped, and endeavour to do the same for others. It's not about feeling gratitude towards the people who helped you along the way – this goes without saying – but to truly repay the debt, you need to extend a helping hand to people to whom you owe nothing.

I will never forget the months Wendy and I spent in the US, travelling on Greyhound buses along the East Coast, and from Ohio to Texas, asking store owners whether we could work in their shops for a few days, getting to know all aspects of their business. It was the most transformative experience of my life, not only because of what I learnt, but also because of the generosity of the American store owners, not one of whom turned us away. It taught me to never become too big or too busy to see anyone who requested a bit of my time.

Here are a few simple strategies to gather new viewpoints, soak up fresh ideas and generally keep one step ahead (with grasshoppers sticking out of your ears!):

Listening & observing rather than talking and instructing. Sometimes the obvious needs to be stated. It is easy to confuse listening with momentary silence, yielded in order for the other person to state their case while we bide our time before restating ours. Real listening means clearing your mind of your preconceived conclusions, and truly taking in and considering what the other person is saying. That said, don't discount your intuition when listening; sometimes it's what people don't say that says the most. And while it is no substitute for first-hand experience or dialogue, opinions and trends picked from the so-called grapevine are worth gathering into the mix.

Reading & research are time-consuming but essential. The best way to pick up trends is to read the financial papers every morning and the weeklies over the weekend. Skim through them to pick up what's relevant to your business and take relevant clippings as you come across them (assuming you still read hard copy!). There are of course many online options as well, some of which are discussed in the Appendix.

Writing both crystallises thoughts and entrenches lessons. I have always believed that gathered information needs to be processed on paper; even when I was a junior haberdashery buyer I would write pages and pages on buttons, or zips, or dress materials, learning

'It is easy to confuse listening with momentary silence. Real listening means clearing your mind of preconceived conclusions, and truly considering what is being said.'

along the way what worked and what didn't. The observing was important but the writing was key – I was observing new things every day, and if I didn't write it down it would disappear, replaced by the next fresh observation or experience. With each day passing I can't remember what I did the day before – unless I record each one.

Dreaming – I think there's much to be said for recording your dreams. I'm not suggesting the kind of obsessive-compulsive dream collection that bores dinner-party guests, but it's worth keeping a pen and paper next to your bed for those dreams in which the subconscious, sifting through the daily debris, suddenly pierces right into conscious thought, and wakes you up with a start. If this happens, jot down the salient points before (with luck!) going back to sleep. Looking at these notes the next morning can sometimes be very illuminating, not in any predictive sense but because you often gain a great deal more insight into your own deep-seated instinctive responses to the situation at hand.

Conferences and seminars – You can certainly learn a lot by attending these, assuming you go with a receptive, open mind. As important as listening to the speakers is the opportunity to mingle with fellow delegates and share trends and stories. Find out which conference is the best in your field (in mine it was the annual CIES conference), and make sure you attend it; if you can afford it, budget for more, and make sure your key employees are similarly exposed.

Consultants are often costly and not necessarily effective. I tend to use them very sparingly, preferring to consult the brainpower around me. However, there are obvious areas of expertise where outside help is enormously beneficial, such as financial planning, tax compliance, IT, marketing and succession planning. There are cheaper ways to access specialist knowledge: your bank can help with financial and estate planning, for instance, or you could approach an advertising school with your company as a marketing project for final-year students, or advertise for interns on a university or college campus. These routes provide fledgling businesses with affordable and creative solutions that may or may not be useful in the long run. But if you are going to spend money on qualified specialists, hire the best your money can buy. Shop around, using sources such as the Internet, Chamber of Commerce, affiliated organisations and magazines specialising

'Don't say you can't afford to travel. See it as a necessary (and tax-deductible) expense, do it on a strict budget, and just get out there.'

in your industry. Interview a number of people and choose the one who strikes a chord with you.

Travel is key to the grasshopper principle. Not leisure travel, but travel to see how your business interest is done elsewhere, in places that are known to be blazing a new trail in your field. Every time Wendy and I went overseas I was like blotting paper, looking at new formats, trying to learn more about how they worked, and why. Before we opened our first hypermarket – one of the most capital-intensive and therefore stressful experiences in my life – I researched them extensively abroad. I knew exactly how much land was required, how near it needed to be to consumers, what size population I needed to pay for it, and so on. I copied it virtually brick by brick. Innovative services, such as offering shoppers the opportunity to make third-party payments, or cash withdrawals, are also imports. Don't say you can't afford to travel. Virtually no one can! Rather see it as a necessary (and tax-deductible) expense, do it on a strict budget, and just get out there. You will pick up an incredible trail of ideas to inspire you.

PRINCIPLE #35

'It's not what you know, but what you do.'

I am often asked why I am so prepared to talk or write about the business model and principles that built Pick 'n Pay. 'Aren't you giving away hard-won ideas? Ways of doing things that will benefit prospective or current competitors?'

I have just never been one of those people who feels protective about his or her knowledge, or tries to hoard his skills. People think that knowledge is so valuable. Why? Knowledge is important, but there is nothing so secret in this world that someone who is prepared to listen and learn cannot discover it.

People who elevate knowledge tend to hoard it, holding their knowledge tightly to their chest. They think that it is their *knowledge* that makes them special, or invaluable, and that is why they must protect it, sometimes even from their own staff! This is not clever. It is, dare I say, rather stupid. Because it's only by sharing your knowledge that everyone can appreciate it, and admire or discard it as they see fit.

Most people tend to be so wrapped up in their own ideas that they don't take that much notice of what others say. They will listen to a conference speaker, and appear to be all fired up, but soon return to their old habits and routines. I can't tell you the number of international conferences I have

'People think that knowledge is so valuable. Why? It's not the clever guys who come first, unless they have the initiative and passion to implement their knowledge.'

attended over the years, discussing the various issues with fellow delegates who left ostensibly full of vim, resolute and earnest, only to meet up with them a year or two later and discover that they have in fact done *absolutely nothing*!

I have met many clever guys who know a great deal more than I do, but it's not the clever guys who come first, unless they have the initiative and passion to *implement* their knowledge. Knowledge is just the beginning: once you have it, you need to be able to act, to '*do*'.

CHAPTER 15

Generosity – Ethics as Enlightened Self-interest

Deciding What to Do

PRINCIPLE #36

'Doing good is good business.'

It was quite something to find myself at a dinner seated next to Milton Friedman, the Nobel prize-winning economist whose views were the antithesis of mine. Conversation was, shall we say, robust. Friedman first made waves in 1970 with an article for *The New York Times Magazine* that led with the headline: 'The Social Responsibility of Business is to Increase Its Profits'. In it Friedman attacked the idea that business 'should promote desirable social ends', have 'a social conscience' or take seriously its responsibilities for providing employment, eliminating discrimination, avoiding pollution 'or whatever else may be the catchwords of the contemporary crop of reformers'. Friedman concluded: 'Businessmen who talk this way are unwitting puppets of the intellectual forces that have been undermining the basis of a free society these past decades.'

Utter hogwash.

I told Friedman as much then. A business built on a deeper purpose may not dominate the economic landscape but it is a long-distance runner in it, outliving flashier outfits built on profit maximisation. But this kind of argument is not won with choice words around a dinner table; the real test takes place in the competitive marketplace. While Pick 'n Pay con-

> *'Most people are basically good, with similar core values. They want to inhabit a moral universe, where integrity and hard work are rewarded.'*

tinues to deliver annual growth, year-on-year, it gives me no great pleasure to say that the blind adherence to Friedman's theories – which in many ways spawned the 'greed is good' mantra of the 1980s and much of the three decades that followed – has been proven to be ruinous to economies and financial markets across the globe.

This is because human nature (aside from a few unhinged individuals) operates on levels other than self-interest and greed. Humans require empathy, friendship and social approval. A 'profit-maximisation' business model does nothing to tap into these powerful motivators.

Since the collapse of financial markets in 2008, 'ethical corporate governance' has finally become more than just a buzzword, and has been shoehorned into business degrees. But anyone can write a document setting out a corporation's approach and commitment to ethical governance. A company has to live by this ethos, and this only happens when the leader prioritises an ethical approach throughout his or her dealings, bringing it to bear in every business decision. This is not about being an 'unwitting puppet of intellectual forces' or a social 'reformer'. 'Enlightened self-interest' is the phrase that I think best captures the reason for, and the power of, acting with a social conscience and investing in social responsibility. Amazingly, despite being vital to the long-term success of any endeavour, this concept is often entirely overlooked.

PRINCIPLE #37

'Conduct every relationship with integrity.'

Aside from wanting to belong to an organisation that they feel proud of, people want to belong to a place where they feel secure, with a strict ethical code of conduct that governs everyone's behaviour within it.

I believe most people are basically good, with similar core values, and that, ideally, they *want* to inhabit a moral universe, where integrity and hard work are rewarded, and no one receives special favours or promotions because of who they know or where they stand in the hierarchy. Strict rules governing ethics create a safe place where everyone knows where they stand. Of course, the dominant values inherent in various organisations may differ, but here are a few that should be inviolate.

The way you live your personal life will in time affect your business life, and vice versa, so *conduct all your relationships – business and personal – with integrity*. Always

*'Too many people think they can live off
their business; they take in increments, then
act surprised when their staff follow suit.'*

standing by your word is the root of that essential ingredient
in any long-term relationship: trust.

I think most people understand the basic rule of ownership: *you don't take something that doesn't belong to you.*
And yet how muddied the water gets in the workplace! I tried
to keep things simple by never confusing my needs with
those of the company. I charged every newspaper and magazine to my own account, as I did my private calls, my lunch-
eons, my family trips – absolutely everything I personally
consumed. I probably erred on the over-cautious side, but
too many people think they can live off their business; they
take in increments, then act surprised when their staff follow
suit, pilfering bits and pieces to which they feel entitled. As
stated in Chapter 10: do not see the business as your personal belonging. Identify it as a third party, totally separate
from you, to which you have no more entitlement than any
other employee. Do this, and you will have created a clear
moral universe for your employees to work within, with a far
healthier business as a result.

I have similarly strong feelings about gifts: *if you cannot reciprocate, don't accept.* Or, as the cliché goes, lunch
paid for by someone else is seldom free. I'm not suggesting
a churlish or panicked reaction to tokens of appreciation,
such as a bottle of champagne at the end of the year, but

we all know when we are being 'wooed'. It is a pleasant feeling, of course, and all too easy to get caught up in the attention.

If someone takes you out for lunch, it is pretty simple to return the favour, but guard against larger overtures. Accepting a gift of value, such as a ticket to an important sports game, or small but frequent gifts, will link you to the giver, and it can become very hard to extricate yourself. We all know what happens next: owing favours corrupts the natural decision-making process; what should be an objective weighing of pros and cons is now coloured by debt. This is all pretty first-base thinking, but again it is amazing how many owners expect their staff to remain inviolate from inappropriate gestures that could be described as bribery yet seem to feel they are exempt from the same rules. You can hardly expect your staff to reject gifts if you are not seen to do the same.

'If you have been swindled, do not be swayed by prior loyalties and how much you may have valued that person: no one is irreplaceable.'

If leading with integrity creates a moral universe where employees feel safe, so too is a ruthless response to any corrupting influence. Act fast and remove the problem. The punishment must fit the crime; someone pilfering for their own gain must be fired, while someone caught stealing information for the competition should be charged and prosecuted in a court of law. If you have been swindled, do not be swayed by prior loyalties and how much you may have valued that person: no one is irreplaceable. Having said that I will do anything to stay out of court, there comes a time when this is the only way to settle a dispute. The vicious court case I fought against John Lawley, my chief buyer, who copied confidential documents to share with a competitor and tried to pinch ten of my key staff, cost me emotionally. He had been my stalwart, a man I thought I could trust with anything. I would have given him anything, but he sold me out to the first competitor who waved a big chequebook around. When the ruling finally came, he lost everything, including the right to work anywhere in the retail industry again, which is what he was best at. When he surreptitiously broke the court order, working for a small retailer, I went for him again, even though he offered no direct competition to me. It was tough and unpleasant to persecute this man I had once trusted, with whom I shared so many memories and had so loved working with. My family, seeing how deeply the whole affair upset me – even affecting my ability to run my business at the time – urged me to drop the second case, to just 'let it go', but it was a matter of principle. I wanted everyone to know that dishonesty and disloyalty on this scale would never be tolerated in my organisation. No one wanted to end up like Lawley: defeated, humiliated and penniless.

PRINCIPLE #38

'Tithe yourself.'

I am not in favour of the parsimonious, neither of the flamboyant. I have always wanted to do well in life, but money was never part of my ambition, and I have always resisted friends for whom it is. There is so much poverty in the world, particularly in this country, that it just seems wrong to wave your good fortune around and make a fuss about it.

There is no doubt that it is good for your spiritual health to share; some, particularly those living under the conditional covenant of the Old Testament or Koran, believe in giving away 10% of their income to their church or a chosen charity, but you can set the 'tithe' as high or low as you like.

There seems little point in waiting until you're dead before sharing your wealth with your family, or those whose children are hungry, or the elderly and penniless. Be calm, be generous and give wisely. As important as it is to give is the motive behind the gift. Give of yourself (not just money) intelligently and with good grace. Your spiritual health is as important as your physical, emotional and financial wellbeing. Exercise it regularly, or part of you will wither.

CHAPTER 16

Marketing From the Heart

How to Get Noticed Without Spending a Fortune

PRINCIPLE #39

'Don't buy PR, live it.'

I was hugely excited about visiting the Schwegmann store, at the time the biggest supermarket in the world; the 14 400-square-metre New Orleans building attracted almost as many tour buses as it did shoppers. I was equally exhilarated by the prospect of meeting the legendary grocer himself – anyone who made statements like, 'There are richer and smarter people in the world than I am, but they're no better' and 'We're all of us selling something to someone else', was a man after my own heart. So I was a little nonplussed to arrive in town to find he'd been arrested, with photos of him behind bars splashed across the newspapers and posters.

So commenced my first lesson in guerrilla marketing, although I believe the phrase – denoting unconventional ways to showcase your business that cost little or nothing – was only coined later.

John F Schwegmann had revolutionised grocery shopping in New Orleans; he introduced self-service shopping, incentivising shoppers by offering a 10% discount if they helped themselves (much as companies today offer a discount to people who shop or make their bookings online, or banks who penalise people who use cashiers and cheques rather than ATMs and EFTs). He was one of the early retailers to stock big volumes in order to reduce mark-ups, famously stating that he 'would rather make $100 off $1 000 in sales than make $50 on $100 sales'.

I had heard that Schwegmann was a maverick, but I hadn't realised just how much he liked a good fight when he thought his customers were being short-changed.

Schwegmann – who'd recently had a law that required a minimum mark-up on all alcohol overturned as 'unconstitutional' – had been arrested for buying milk from outside the state of Louisiana. He'd been purchasing it from farmers in a neighbouring state because it was cheaper there, and passing the savings on to his customers. The Louisiana Milk Commission, who set local milk prices, weren't having it. They fined him twice – the second fine was $1 000, quite a substantial amount at the time – but Schwegmann just kept 'importing' his milk. On the day we arrived in town, the Louisiana health officials had just impounded his entire milk consignment, and the Milk Commission had moved to prosecute. That was a bad mistake, with a fallout I witnessed first-hand.

Schwegmann's retaliation – ads in the local papers and posters of himself behind bars, announcing that he would stop at nothing to break the Milk Commission's monopoly on prices – paid off handsomely: customers flooded his store in active support. A federal suit went into litigation for eight years, but Schwegmann finally won the case, and the Milk Commission was disbanded shortly thereafter. Aside from the publicity he won for his stores, public support was such that

Schwegmann was elected to the state legislature. And all it cost him was a couple of fines.

At the time I was – and remain – virulently anti-monopoly, but it was Schwegmann who gave me the confidence to wage a similar kind of war back home. It wasn't entirely risk-free; if Schwegmann had lost his litigation battles, it would have cost him dearly, but he hated the ridiculous injustice, the sheer waste of restricting trade at the expense of ordinary people. His belligerence in the face of a law that was literally milking the public exhilarated and inspired me, knowing as I did how many similar price-fixing monopolies existed in South Africa, where the public could afford it even less.

Fighting for the right to provide the most affordable goods possible was not the only lesson that Schwegmann taught me. He also showed me how presentation (or lack thereof) can be as important an influencer as price. 'Take a look at this, Ackerman,' he barked, sticking out his stocky right arm and deftly rolling up his sleeve. Schwegmann shoved his elbow under my nose, revealing flesh that was mottled in deep purple and various shades of yellow. I looked sympathetic, wondering what the hell was going on. Schwegmann winked at me. 'Watch ...' He strode up to the end of one of his aisles, where tinned merchandise was stacked in a classic pyramid. With a deliberate swagger, Schwegmann jabbed his elbow straight into the stack, sending the tins flying. Quick as a flash, he was back with me. 'Now look,' he said, 'watch 'em fly off the floor.' He was right: housewives walking past stopped to pick up a tin, turned it around, then put it in

> *'No business exists in a vacuum. Whatever you are selling, you are working for, and within, a community.'*

their trolley before moving on. Schwegmann chuckled. 'See, Ackermann, if the ends are stacked too neat and high, the women won't touch 'em. Most of the ladies who come in here are real house-proud, and they don't want to make something that looks so neat, look messy. So I do it!' In recent years I have come across the phrase 'nudge marketing', referring to the more subtle ways in which marketers influence consumers, but it was Schwegmann and his elbow who showed it to me first!

Schwegmann opened my mind to the creative ways in which you can serve your customers, and the power of publicity when you stand up and fight for their rights. At the root of his fight against price monopolies was his sense of responsibility towards his community. Today no-one discounts that social responsibility programmes should be part of your overall marketing plan, but in times of economic stress social responsibility is often the first thing people choose to cut back on. This is a mistake. Social responsibility is not only integral to promoting your company; it should be part of your business plan, as important as your staff, your administration and your product – the third Leg of a strong table.

PRINCIPLE #40

'The more you give away profits, the more the money flows back.'
– Gottlieb Duttweiler

If you're just starting out and have a tiny advertising or PR budget, don't fret. Aside from being a larger-than-life Schwegmann character, there are very effective ways of building PR.

No business exists in a vacuum. Whether you are supplying dresses, loans, laundry services, air conditioners, books, medical supplies, gardens, beds – anything! – you are working for, and within, a community. It may not be an entirely homogeneous community, but it is still a group (or groups) that can be defined either by geography or demographics, or by the interests or purpose of its members.

An integral part of the third Leg is to actively show your community spirit. Without fail, every community has needs that are not being met due to funding shortfalls or lack of interest, capacity or time. Find out what these are and act on them. Finding out where a community needs support is not difficult: if most of your customers are parents, you can be sure that every one of their children's schools will need help with fundraising; every community has grandparents who may require assistance; most have places of worship that welcome any help (be careful to spread this across all faiths so as to not alienate any particular group of custom-ers); if your customers are sport-lovers there will be clubs and events that need support; there may be neglected open spaces or parks near your business premises; and so on. Don't just stick to helping a group of people you identify with; try to move through an entire community group by group, month by month – becoming aware of the social problems around you in the process. Don't forget your employees are also part of a community – don't ignore the social responsibilities that are close to their hearts.

Getting involved need not require a huge financial com-mitment; even a tiny business, newly launched, stands to gain by showing its commitment in some way. This can be as small as offering your product as part of the prize line-up in a local school auction to spending a Sunday morning working a church bazaar stall. In fact, offering up some time or exper-tise can be far more effective than a mere cash donation, and will teach you more about the community at large, which you in turn could see as market research – the 'win–win' situation that sales people love to go on about.

It is never more important to show this commitment than when disaster strikes unexpectedly. Be at the forefront to help; whether it's handing out blankets or cups of tea, facilitating collection points, raising awareness or making donations, make sure your business or brand is associated with being ac-tively caring in times of distress. Do not concern yourself with the cost; the customer support you gain may not by quantifi-able but it will be huge.

Aside from the personal pleasure you will experience by

doing something constructive (and believe me, this is not to be underestimated), no amount of costly advertising can ever match the positive association and goodwill this kind of community involvement will create for your business.

PRINCIPLE #41

'Acts of kindness build a business.'

Aside from the impact the spirit of 'doing good' has on prospective customers, it has an inestimable effect on your employees. Make sure they and their communities are aware of, and part of, the process, and they will feel immense pride in belonging to an organisation that is seen by their family and friends as concerned and caring. By association, they too feel a force for good, and are often inspired to become even more actively involved within the community, creating a knock-on effect that is immensely gratifying.

To further encourage this civic-minded spirit within our organisation, Pick 'n Pay managers in the Northern region created an award system called the WOWs, in which we celebrate the many random acts of kindness practised by Pick 'n Pay staff: the manager who put two of his staff through university; the employee who went out of his way to help a customer with a puncture, enabling her to get to an im-

'An organisation that is actively seen to care and act in the interests of its staff and community will never lose customers to the competition.'

portant meeting on time; the staff member who noticed a woman going into labour on her way home and stopped to stay with her and call an ambulance; or the group of 15 at one of our stores who get together every second Sunday to help out at an old-age home – mowing the lawns, making Sunday lunch, reading aloud. It would be impossible to list all of the wonderful acts of kindness by the caring individuals that we are so grateful to count as members of the Pick 'n Pay family. The point is that not one of them is specifically aimed at gaining customers but rather at serving the larger community, individual by individual.

To demonstrate the knock-on effect of noticing and encouraging this community spirit: when we started the award, we celebrated 560 WOW awards; within a few years this figure soon grew to in excess of 1 000 – small yet heroic acts of caring that we celebrate every year at a special award ceremony in Pretoria. I don't care if it's good economics or bad economics according to the prevalent fashion in the business lecture rooms, these acts of kindness build a business. An organisation that is actively seen to care and act in the interests of its staff and community will never lose customers to the competition.

PRINCIPLE #42

'Real stories inspire.'

Over the years I have regaled people with the story of how I told my driver to 'Follow that car!' when I spotted a woman driving with a back seat full of Checkers bags, and followed her all the way home to ask her why she wasn't shopping with us. Or how, because I have always given strict instructions that customer calls be put straight through to me, I lost out on a big property deal because the guys lost patience listening to me placate an irate customer who was unhappy about her cottage cheese purchase. Or the time I set alight a consignment of coffin-shaped pencil boxes, much to the delight of the customer who had complained about them. But the stories that personally delight me are those that involve my staff, such as the article that appeared in the press about Sam Tsukudu, a Pick 'n Pay worker who was photographed carrying home a frail, elderly gentleman who had collapsed on the way home because he had missed his bus. In the article, Sam, who also regularly walks a blind shopper home and helps unpack his groceries, is celebrated for his community spirit.

Stories like this do more to illustrate our commitment to consumer sovereignty than any placard or open letter ever will. That's not to say any of the stories unfolded simply because I wanted to retell them one day; they happened the way they did because I have always tried to live my mission statement. They truly reflect the way I feel, and am. This goes back to one of my earlier points: if you feel your mission statement acutely and passionately, you too will build up a story bank that you can draw on to illustrate your commitment – a far more powerful motivator than a clever advertising headline or once-off promotion. It is in essence the difference between 'editorial' and 'advertorial'; 'editorial' is not only free but is also a hundred times more powerful because it is read, heard and talked about; advertorial, which is simply advertising dressed up like editorial, costs money and, even if well-conceived, will never be as noticed or believed as a real story.

Essential to any story is, of course, the storyteller. I have always enjoyed a good relationship with journalists. In the weeks following the announcement of my imminent retirement, I was overwhelmed again by how positive and rewarding this relationship has been. The press has always been darn good to me, and I appreciate this, knowing how much easier it is to find fault than to flatter. Perhaps it is also because I have always treated every journalist I have ever encountered with the same courtesy and respect I accord customers and employees. No matter how busy I am, or how junior the reporter, or how small the publication, I always return their calls, stand up when they enter, shake hands with sincerity, offer them lunch if that's the time of day, and generally go out of my way to make them feel at ease. I am shocked when I hear of journalists being treated with disdain. If everyone is a potential customer, if every person holds the potential to add another positive testimonial to your PR arsenal, how much more so someone who has the power to reproduce your stories in the free press? Aside from this basic common sense, there is a good chance that the cub reporter at a community paper will one day find herself posted as senior editor at one of the country's financial dailies; that reporter might remember the kindness and respect shown to her as a junior, and over the years could write a number of flattering articles that will reinforce positive perceptions that will, in turn, help sustain your share price. And all it would have cost was a smile and twenty minutes of your time.

CHAPTER 17

Hope –
The Importance
of Optimism

Positive Attitude Equals
Positive Bottom Line

PRINCIPLE #43

'Leaders deal in hope.'

Attitudes are contagious. Yours is thus critical. Are you a glass-half-full or a glass-half-empty kind of person? If the latter, you need to sit down and reassess that glass.

I believe everyone has the capacity to lead, if leadership is defined as having a clear goal, an achievable plan and the desire to energise others to get you there. But key to getting where you want to go is your outlook.

I simply cannot stress enough the importance of being positive. It may even be *the* most important ingredient in a successful business – not only essential in the '90% guts' prerequisite for starting a venture, but directly affecting everything that follows. From your relationship with yourself to dealing with staff, suppliers and customers, you need to stay enthusiastic, to be able to persevere despite routine setbacks, as every part feeds into the cycle that results in your bottom line.

Of course it is not easy being positive all the time, particularly if you are not that way inclined, or recovering from one of the unfair knocks that life deals out from time to time. When I was in my twenties and thirties, I thought I was immune from these knocks. I worked hard; I ran a reasonably good show. I thought knocks were reserved for people who were floundering and failing, the ones who needed a bit of a knock to sort them out. Then I got tossed out like a dirty rag, and I understood fully for the first time just how random these knocks could be. It is easy to become cynical after an experience like this, but cynicism is counterproductive. I opted rather to become canny, not in any devious sense, but in the sense of being wiser to what I really wanted from life, and how to get it.

Life is harder if you are, deep down, suspicious of human nature. 'People are good until proven otherwise', is the far healthier position. Of course, not everyone understands the value of this. Some see the world as a rough, tough place where nice guys come last. The world is tough but that does

> *'The world is tough but that does not mean you have to be.'*

not mean you have to be. Steel does not have to be sheathed in steel. Besides, I'm not suggesting you take on an irritating 'jolly hockey sticks' mentality, or kid yourself when faced with bad news, or hide from an intuitive sense that a situation is unstable or a certain person untrustworthy. Being positive does not preclude you from being a realist. But for many people the urge to complain, criticise and dwell on the negative is the default position. If this is you, snap out of it!

PRINCIPLE #44

'Don't let the sun set on a problem.'

Being positive is not a lucky disposition that only some are born with, but an attitude anyone can actively cultivate. As the cliché goes: it's not the cards you're dealt, but how you play them, that counts. When you feel yourself falling into a negative state, stop to meticulously analyse the situation you are in, trying to understand the real causes of the negative state, before working on solutions (as described in Chapters 1 and 2). Whatever you do, don't leave a problem to fester, or ruminate on old setbacks. Take control by banishing old and painful associations, immediately replacing them with more recent, positive memories. Immediate problems need concrete steps to remedy them. Don't give up. Only considered action will make you feel like you are in control, and control is crucial to confidence.

Of course, there are aspects beyond our control that can negatively impact on our emotional wellbeing: the ill health of a loved one, global recession, divorce. Hard as it is, the things you have no control over must not be allowed to sap you. For some, the so-called Serenity Prayer works as a mantra. Penned by German theologian Reinhold Niebuhr in the 1930s and appropriated by Alcoholics Anonymous (AA) some years later, it reads: 'God grant me the serenity to accept the

'An objective and thorough analysis of most events will enable you to glean a positive view – the so-called silver lining, elusive but always there.'

things I cannot change; the courage to change the things that I can; and the wisdom to know the difference.' Bear in mind that an objective and thorough analysis of most events will enable you to glean a positive view – the so-called silver lining, elusive but always there.

Aside from actively cultivating your own positive attitude, be vigilant against negative emotions flourishing amongst your staff.

It is of vital import to balance criticism with a positive outlook when providing feedback, be it a one-on-one staff performance feedback or a board meeting dealing with quarterly figures; *always* start the meeting by listing the positive achievements, rather than just launching into negatives or criticism. A diatribe may be a way to vent pent-up stress, but what does it contribute to staff morale?

While a certain amount of gossip is inevitable, leaders should actively discourage colleagues criticising each other behind their backs. Make it very clear that should someone have a problem with a fellow employee, they will receive a fair hearing should they discuss the matter with you – but individually, and in private. Do not allow criticism to be bandied about in groups unless the person is present and able to defend him- or herself. There is a kind of pack mentality that can settle into a group criticising an absent colleague, which I find very disturbing. It can kill relationships stone-dead, and is a poison in the company well, as the trust between colleagues starts to atrophy. Tackle it immediately and try to resolve the problem; if all else fails, you will have to lose one of them, because nothing affects company mentality as adversely as warring factions within the organisation.

PRINCIPLE #45

'Live life as an optimist.'

Countless studies have proven that optimists not only enjoy life and achieve, but they live much longer!

Living in a country that appears to be beset with problems can drain enthusiasm for enterprise. This is a pity. Unlike many of those who find little good to say about the state of our nation, I am (regrettably!) old enough to remember graphically the sheer awfulness of life in South Africa during the closing decades of the last century, not to mention the iniquitous laws that led to the violence and insecurity of those times. Even in our darkest hour, I never lost my faith that South Africa would one day emerge from its long apartheid night into a dawn filled with vibrant promise. The truly extraordinary thing about our present isn't the array of prob-

'Actively discourage colleagues criticising each other behind their backs. A kind of pack mentality can settle in, which I find very disturbing.'

lems confronting us but how far we have come from that day in 1994 when every South African finally cast his or her vote.

I have no hesitation in saying that South Africa is a far, far better place today, and while our problems are pretty daunting, they are not ours alone. It's true that the heady idealism that followed the first democratic election has been corroded by government's inability to impact significantly on the lot of the impoverished, the homeless and the sick, but there is nothing to be gained from pessimism. The entrepreneur in particular must not lose faith. Opportunity exists everywhere for those prepared to look. As the American journalist Ambrose Bierce wrote, cynicism is dangerous, because it sees things as they were, or are, not as they can or should be. Do not yield to the caustic voices of those who argue that the best is not possible; it is – but first you need to visualise it.

CHAPTER 18

Stand Still and You're Dead

Why You Need to Keep Changing

PRINCIPLE #46

'You can't be in business today with yesterday's methods, and expect to be in business tomorrow.'

They say the only person who likes change is a baby with a wet nappy. I certainly don't like it. Change is difficult. It takes effort, it usually costs and it feels risky. But change we must.

If you are successful, others will follow. Some will try to steal your ideas, others your staff; mostly they will want your customers. Don't wait for them to catch up before you act. Embrace change as an integral part of your leadership. No matter how well you are doing, you cannot ever afford to stand still; maintaining a static position and hoping that the good times will keep flowing is like closing your eyes and hoping no one can see you – naive.

It's not just competitors who keep changing the rules. Factors such as the economic climate, innovations in technology, environmental pressure, labour influx, tax laws – in short, the ever-evolving landscape in which we operate – mean we have to keep anticipating and changing just to maintain our current impetus, never mind expand and grow.

I once had a director who, after an exceptional set of annual results, said: 'We're obviously doing something right; if it ain't broke, let's not fix it!' I felt like firing him on the spot (I didn't!). But that kind of attitude is the death knell to

> 'When business is peaking, that is exactly
> the time to invest heavily, because you
> have the cash flow to do so.'

progress. When business is peaking, that is exactly the time to invest heavily, because you have the cash flow to do so. And rest assured, the times they are a-changing, and innovations you don't know about are being hatched by competitors both known and new. There are always better ways to do things; make sure you are the one doing them. Because waiting for a reason to change – a new competitor, a sustained price war, a steady drop-off in sales – is often too late.

With success comes increasing pressure to grow. You need to grow to satisfy demand, to keep the best employees exhilarated and committed, and to increase your buying power and negotiating clout, which in turn ultimately lowers prices and attracts more numbers to a growing customer base. Growth strategies usually comprise your acquiring another business or premises, being acquired by a bigger operation, franchising, going public or innovating. Bar innovating, almost all options carry the risk of losing control of the company, as any kind of expansion requires access to capital. It's a vicious circle, and you will need to tread carefully when faced with this pressure.

At this stage it is worth asking yourself again: 'Why am I in business?'

If exponential growth will no longer provide the right answer, then your mission statement is probably ill served, and you may want to reign in an aggressive expansion programme that will ultimately dilute your distinctiveness, or *raison d'être*. If the idea of a big capital outlay makes you nervous (and understandably so), you don't have to physically expand your operation. Don't pursue growth for the sake of it. However, this is not an invitation to let the business stagnate. You will still need to innovate and modernise your existing outfit, offering new services, new products or a new or refurbished environment. The latter is particularly important in the retail industry: we have learnt from experience that stores need to be renovated every seven years or sales start to lag; without fail, stores record phenomenal growth after refurbishment.

Look also at creating innovative new formats. Having expanded my supermarkets nationally, I wanted a new challenge. I knew the consumer market was still largely untapped, and quickly moved to be the one to build South Africa's first hypermarket. Having established hypermarkets, I then wanted to be the first to create superstores, then family stores, and so on. I constantly scoured the world for new formats and products to keep my customers excited.

This is why you need to feel passionate about your business, because it needs to occupy your mind in the spaces left between running it – the creative places, where you can free associate and develop new ways of presenting your product or service.

The pace of change is crucial. Expanding too quickly can kill a business quicker than staying static. Set a pace you can afford – both financially and mentally. Do not be 'bullied' into doing something that your gut warns you may be premature

'Most growth strategies carry the risk of losing control of the company, as expansion requires access to capital. At this stage it is worth asking yourself again: "Why am I in business?"'

or wrong. Some years back, when we had identified a need to diversify, possibly offshore, I was almost persuaded to invest in a chain of stores in Los Angeles, but the more I was rushed and pushed, the more I dug in, insisting I needed time to consider the deal. If the 'bargain' I was being harassed to purchase was picked up by someone less hesitant, they were welcome to it. There is seldom a good reason to rush into a decision this big, and I am glad I stuck to my guns, finally deciding against it, and avoided what would have been a toxic decision.

PRINCIPLE #47

'Business practices may change, but principles must remain.'

Before you make any changes to your business, be it to simply modernise your existing operations or a radical new expansion plan, remember always to differentiate between business practices and values. Business practices – the way you operate your business – need to be reinvented constantly, but your business principles – those values on which you have built your business – must remain intact.

The bigger the company grows, the more tempting it is to drop the foundation values, particularly if they are deemed 'old-fashioned' or 'too expensive' to maintain. Don't do it. The values that build a business – be it an overarching desire to serve, or specifically to innovate, or to pursue the best quality, or the best price – are timeless and transcendent; they define our business and tell us who we are. They are what give you and your business integrity. They are, in a word, sacred.

PRINCIPLE #48

'Profits are more important than market share.'

There is a great deal more sense in ensuring that each of your outlets, divisions or stores is profitable, rather than pouring energy and money into extending market share, even if this will in the short term affect your share value. To me, the question is not, 'How big is your operation?' All I want to know is, 'Are you making money?'

It's common sense really, but many companies don't

understand this, equating 'largest market share' with some kind of triumph over competitors. In the 1980s, Checkers displayed a classic case of this ill-conceived drive to dominate the market, which they did – almost putting themselves out of business in the process.

However, if it doesn't adversely affect profits, expanding market share makes sense. But, as discussed above, expansion plans cost money. There are the same routes you would have investigated when you first had to raise capital (see Chapter 5), but with an established business you have more options, such as going public or franchising your operation. Whichever route you take, make sure you don't lose control of the business. If the only way to raise the cash means you will lose control, then be prepared to become an employee in the company you created ... Better, perhaps, to sell the business in its entirety than suffer this ignominy.

Assuming your business is worth a million or more, and turns over in excess of R500 000, going public is an excellent way to raise additional capital – again, unless you lose control of the company in the process. When the idea of going public was mooted by my brother as part of his final-year thesis, my company was only a year old, but his proposal, albeit theoretical, struck a chord. I had a major price war with Checkers on my hands, so the need to expand was rather pressing.

There was, however, a major problem: having given away a large batch of shares upfront to start the company – almost 40% – going public would mean that I would lose my controlling share.

'If raising cash means losing control, then be prepared to become an employee in the company you created.'

One of my legal advisers, a very astute man, devised what can only be described as an audacious proposal. Calling all the existing shareholders together, he described the situation to them: that unless we raised additional capital to expand the company nationally, the price war would kill us, and that an effective solution would be to go public, but that this would mean that I would lose control of the company. Everyone knew how passionate I was about the company; taking away control would mean that I wouldn't be able to make key decisions without lengthy consultations. No one wanted an ineffective and demoralised leader at the helm. So my lawyer suggested that the company go public, but – if the shareholders agreed – I would in the process get a larger chunk as we floated: for every two shares each current shareholder automatically received, I would receive four. Amazingly, the shareholders agreed. I in turn delivered: R100 invested in the business upon listing in 1968 would today be worth about R1 million – a compound annual growth of 25.3%.

If you have a concept that is franchisable, this is another potential way to raise capital, though again you will need enough capital to invest in marketing the brand to make it desirable to the franchisee, who will want a real return on his or her investment. This is the subject of another book, but if you go this route make sure you do so in such a way that the brand values and mission are upheld.

I believe the Pick 'n Pay franchise model is one of the best in the world precisely because we are not greedy. We opted to make the franchisee king, so that he would be motivated to continue treating our customers as queens. We did this by asking for a mere 1% of profits (others require up to 10%). It's true that franchisees then buy around 90% of their goods from us, but we openly declare what we make on buying. In essence, the model is built on putting the best interests of the franchisee on the table, not profits; all we require is that the franchisee then puts the customer on the top of his (or her) table. As a result, the franchise operations are one of the greatest cash cows for Pick 'n Pay, while simultaneously producing enormous profits for almost all of our franchisees, who in turn are delivering a much improved service to their customers, some of them in far-flung locales all over southern Africa.

CHAPTER 19

Make Mistakes, Not Regrets

Welcoming Adversity

PRINCIPLE #49

'When you come to a roadblock, take the detour.' – Mary Kay Ash

We all shoulder problems more often than we'd like.

The thing is not to feel burdened by them, but to see every one as a puzzle to which you have the key. There is *always* a solution. It may not be the solution you want, but it is – if you apply yourself – the best at hand, a solution in which you understand full well both the circumstances surrounding it and the consequences of taking it.

Deceptively simple but immensely effective, the '7 Tried & True' I discussed in Chapter 2 have remained a key tool of mine in dealing with adversity. The questions remain 'what, where, why, when, which, how and who'; the full phrasing will depend on the kind of problem you're facing, be it an intransigent landlord, concerns about a new venture, decision to upgrade, and so on. Essentially, applying the '7 Tried & True' opens your mind to new angles, allowing you to *reframe the problem*, and in such a way that solutions fall into place. I have included a few examples of how you can

'There is always a solution. It may not be the one you want, but it is – if you apply yourself – the best at hand.'

apply the '7 Tried & True' at the end of the chapter. And remember, should you err and follow a route that fails, this should in no way deter you.

PRINCIPLE #50

'What good is warmth without cold to give it sweetness?' – John Steinbeck

Dealing with adversity is never pleasant. But emotional setbacks plumb the depths of your inner strength: you will never know just how resilient you are until you come face to face with real adversity.

I didn't have a tough life economically, but emotionally it wasn't easy. My parents' acrimonious divorce and custody battle – in which I, aged seven, was coached by my father's lawyer's to denounce my mother in court in her presence – wounded me deeply. Being the only Jew in a Christian school, and subject to anti-Semitic sentiments from certain classmates and teachers, was difficult. Being fired was unpleasant. But the adverse circumstances of my youth and early career defined how I would deal with adversity later in life: by getting up and getting on with it – a survivor's attitude I came to appreciate in later life.

Similar to rising above adversity is transcending your mis-

'You will never know just how resilient you are until you come face to face with real adversity.'

takes. If you can shed your wounded pride, mistakes are the source of life's greatest lessons.

The principle is well distilled in the story, penned anonymously, that runs like this:

'Sir, What is the secret of your success?' the reporter asked the bank president.

'Two words.'

'And, Sir, what are they?'

'Right decisions.'

'And how do you make right decisions?'

'One word.'

'And, Sir, what is that?'

'Experience.'

'And how do you get experience?'

'Two words.'

'And, Sir, what are they?'

'Wrong decisions.'

People make mistakes when they do things for the wrong reasons – chasing money, fearing failure, looking for approbation, wanting the limelight. Whatever the reason, do not burden yourself with loathsome chastisement. Mistakes are easy to analyse in retrospect, but life needs to be lived forward.

I'm no longer entirely sure what the reason was – fear of the future perhaps – but the decision to invest in Australia in 1979, when the world's antagonism towards South Africa was building, was not my brightest moment. I thought the fact that we had Australian partners, were hiring Australian architects and builders, as well as retaining all our Australian staff, would conquer the negative perceptions many Australians had towards South Africa. A few years later, I had to leave with my tail between my legs. It was a mistake I almost compounded when I bought a run-down Australian chain fifteen years later. But I believe that if you truly want something, you don't give up. So I got to know the operation and the staff at grassroots level until I felt the tipping point. I persuaded the board to invest another AU$50 million in the ailing business – one of the gutsier moments in my career – a decision that finally saw the business turn around in the latter half of 2009.

Other than my trying ventures Down Under, I have on occasions made the mistake of opening too many stores in a single catchment area, which meant that existing outlets suffered in the process. But my greatest regrets are the mistakes I made with people, particularly in the early years. In a spectacular run of bad judgment, I hired the wrong person to run Pick 'n Pay in every new province we launched in! The worst thing about this kind of mistake is that it impacts on the very person you wanted to reward. Have the courage to correct this kind of mistake as quickly as you can; if you're not sure, give it a maximum three-month trial run, then move decisively for the sake of all concerned. Those

'Mistakes are easy to analyse in retrospect, but life needs to be lived forward.'

early years taught me to be much more circumspect about judging capacity before promoting someone with enthusiasm alone to a senior management position.

Some mistakes I made I was lucky enough not to have to pay for. In retrospect, I should have pulled out of Trust Bank when that institution's future hung in the balance, but if I had I doubt the bank would have survived. Out of loyalty I didn't withdraw a cent. It was a gamble, and it could have resulted in the biggest mistake of my career; if Trust Bank had gone broke, Pick 'n Pay would have been gone too. By remaining loyal to the banker who had helped me when I started, with a few discounts and so on, I risked my company and the livelihood of thousands. My loyalty to the company should have come first.

I could go on about the small and not-so-small errors inevitable in a four-decade career, but I think it's better to emphasise how much easier it is to deal with potential mistakes, and how much more fun it can be dealing with adversity, when sharing the experience with a professional.

PRINCIPLE #51

'Don't fear the obvious.'

Having been blessed with an intelligent and intuitive life partner, and a generally positive disposition, I would never have believed that I could benefit from, or would in fact enjoy, any form of psychological guidance. But I was wrong.

Genus Resources, the Boston-based company I approached some years back to assist me with my succession planning, suggested that a family consultant might prove beneficial. I never looked back.

I have had an executive coach since 1995. Essentially, an executive coach is there to focus on your career and professional life, helping you to reframe your perspective on work issues. Knowing how unhealthy it is for company morale to discuss colleagues with other colleagues, particularly if you are the boss, it is a great help to have an objective yet interested party to turn to for guidance. A coach will also help you identify your weaknesses, and help clarify the *real* issues at stake, rather than those seen through the prism of your subjective experience. Coaches also help you work with others' perceptions of you – real or imagined.

If you are interested in acquiring the services of one, shop around. I am always in favour of word-of-mouth recommendations, but there is plenty of choice online too; take the time to meet a few before embarking on what is ideally a very rewarding, long-term relationship. Be careful, though: once you have found a coach that works for you, be wary of turning him or her into some kind of 'guru'; sift through their advice as you would any other respected expert hired to consult on business matters, taking on board only what resonates within you.

Lastly, it would be churlish of me to say I have regrets when I have been so fortunate. But no life is perfect, and I wish sometimes that I had spent more time with my kids when they were growing up. Having stated how important it is that you feel passionate about your business, don't allow it to cannibalise the rest of your life. In the final chapter, I share some of the ways in which I tried to contain the demands of my business, and balance them with my personal life.

Reframing the Problem: Exercising the '7 Tried & True'

It may not be entirely clear to you how flexible the '7 Tried & True' analysis is when dealing with a variety of problems. Here, then, are a few examples of how to give any problem a thorough workout in order to help you identify the best way forward.

Problem #1: 'I am struggling to get money owed to me in fast enough to pay my expenses/creditors on time.'

1. What *is the real problem?* I am struggling to bring in money owed because: 1) it is time-consuming; 2) I do not like doing it; 3) creditors are unwilling or unable to pay me any faster; 4) terms are not negotiated upfront; 5) I need a 'policeman' but don't want to alienate my customers. What *do I want to achieve in the short term/ long term?* I want to be able: 1) to standardise payment at no later than 30 days; 2) to not get bogged down in chasing money but free up my time to concentrate on running the business; 3) to not do business with clients who cannot sign up and stick to my conditions. What *will happen if I don't address the problem?* I will go broke.

2. Where *is the problem manifesting itself?* 1) My creditors are losing patience and I am losing any bargaining positioning I had with them; 2) I am anxious about managing cash flow all the time, which is impacting on my performance elsewhere; 3) my bank accounts are in a mess and I cannot negotiate a bigger overdraft; 4) my current overdraft is killing me with interest repayments.

3. Why *is it happening?* 1) Because I haven't invoiced in time or haven't staggered the invoicing; 2) because I don't like asking for money; 3) because

my clients may be experiencing their own cash flow problems; 4) because I have been delivering late.

4. When *should I tackle the problem?* Immediately, or else I will be out of business.

5. Which *solution works best for me?* I need to become more disciplined about 1) negotiating terms upfront; 2) invoicing immediately on completion; 3) insisting that the terms be met, and, if not, taking some kind of punitive action.

6. How *can I best manage/implement the solution?* 1) Hire someone who can assist with negotiating contracts and/or chasing payments? 2) Consider staggered invoicing, with punitive charges for late delivery/payment? 3) Removal of clients who do not honour the payment deadlines?

7. Who *needs to be involved?* An accountant? Banker? Lawyer?

Problem #2: 'I suspect one of my employees is stealing. In every other respect, this employee is excellent. I am not sure what to do.'

1. What *is the real problem?* Stock/money is disappearing. I no longer trust X. **What** *do I want to achieve in the short term/long term?* I want to catch the thief and/or stop the theft.

2. Where *is the problem manifesting itself?* At the back door? In the shop? At the till? On the books?

3. Why *is it happening?* There is a lack of control in my administration/stock management/cash records. The current invoicing and stock/cash intake system is as much at fault as the individual abusing it.

4. When *should I tackle the problem?* Immediately!

5. Which *solution works best for me?* Depending on where the theft is taking place, I need to tighten up my stock management system and cash control. Install CCTV cameras/hire a guard. Confront the employee in order to wring a confession from him/her.

6. How *can I best manage/implement the solution?* Find new ways to cross-check records. (For example, in a guesthouse, records kept by cleaning staff of linen and towel changes will enable the owner to cross-check this against the booking sheet and income.) Threaten the suspected thief with police involvement unless they make a clean confession. If you get a confession, get rid of the employee immediately.

7. Who *needs to be involved?* All my employees. Possibly my accountant, and an HR expert. If necessary, the police.

Problem #3: 'Demand is starting to outstrip my ability to supply. How do I meet this increased demand without compromising the quality that is producing the demand in the first place?'

1. What *is the real problem?* I am experiencing higher demand than I can cope with. I don't like to disappoint customers but I am worried that if I overextend it will impact on my ability to continue delivering my existing quality. I am also worried that, should I ramp up supply, I will lose control of my business. What *do I want to achieve in the short term/long term?* I want to grow my business but not at the expense of my existing customers and reputation. What *will happen if I don't address the problem?* I will lose prospective customers to the competition.

2. Where *is the problem manifesting itself?* Existing customers are disappointed because they want more product/time/contracts. New customers are complaining because they are being turned away. There is tension in the workplace because everyone is stretched to the limit.

3. Why *is it happening?* Lack of equipment? Lack of staff? Lack of training? Lack of space? Unreliable suppliers? Overzealous sales force? Unbalanced marketing?

4. When *should I tackle the problem?* Immediately,

or can I afford to wait? If the latter, how long?

5. Which *solution works best for me?* Should I wait until I have enough profit to grow organically? Or should I raise the capital now?

6. How *can I manage/implement the solution?* If the former, how can I maximise growth without compromising quality or straining/demotivating my workforce due to the increase in pressure? If the latter, should I look at borrowing from the bank/taking on an outside partner(s)/selling to the partners within the company/listing the company?

7. Who *needs to be involved?* My accountant. A venture capitalist? My original investors? The bank? My partner/family? Experts whom I trust?

Problem #4: 'There is chronic conflict between two important staff members, neither of whom I want to lose.'

1. What *is the real problem?* I have two invaluable employees who are struggling to work together. What *do I want to achieve in the short term/long term?* I want to retain both of them as productive members of staff. What *will happen if nothing is done?* 1) Morale will be affected; 2) the company could suffer; 3) I could lose one or both of them.

2. Where *is the problem manifesting itself?*
Tension/badmouthing/undermining. **Where** *can they be redeployed?* I need them both at head office. **Where** *is the best place to work through this problem with the two parties?* Outside of work, in an environment where there are no distractions, for as long as it takes to come up with a solution.

3. Why *is it happening?* Organisational structure? Jealousy? Personality clash? History? My relationship with/attitude towards either?

4. When *should I tackle the problem?* Without delay. **When** *can I let go of the problem?* Once they are working together harmoniously/one of them is gone.

5. Which *kind of approach will work?* Honest, empathetic, decisive. **Which** *kind of result am I looking for?* For them to work through and then set aside their differences and/or to structure organisation in such a way that they complement rather than undermine each other.

6. How *should I manage them/facilitate an agreement? How far should I go?* Listen to both sides of the story. Don't choose sides. Lay the ground rules before bringing them together. Protect both/step in only if disagreement is too heated.

7. Who *needs more assistance/reassurance/is*

more important to the company? List character strengths and weaknesses of both. Decide, if there is no resolution, who finally to back, and dispatch the other with the most generous terms possible.

CHAPTER 20

Time Out – Prioritising

Managing Time

PRINCIPLE #52

'Why waste time climbing mountains when what you really want is to play golf.' – Gus Ackerman

For most of us, there are simply not enough hours in the day.

It is important to work effectively during the hours devoted to business rather than to allow work to increasingly eat into the hours you are supposed to spend at home. Easier said than done, of course. However, as much as I have loved building my business, what I value above all in life is my family. Here, then, are a few ways in which I tried to reduce the impact on my family of my virtually obsessive relationship with Pick 'n Pay. Not always with huge success, it must be admitted ...

> 1. Do not burden yourself with paper at home. Whether it is the financial newspapers or business reports or internal memos, and whether you digest hard copy or read online, try to read business-related work in the office, during lunch hour, on the plane – anywhere but at home. Email is just another kind of work-related 'paper', so switch that function off. Home is the place where you relax, where you engage with family and

'Don't dither. This simply defers the decision, and you will have more to contend with the following day.'

friends and, if you love reading – as I do – where you read books.

2. Make lists. I don't think of myself as a particularly visionary person. What I am good at is setting goals and achieving them. Making 'to do' lists is essential to both. I keep a pocket-sized notebook on hand all the time and add thoughts to the list as soon as they enter my mind. This immediacy is primarily how I manage my time efficiently, because once I have jotted down the concern or idea I can return my full attention to the business at hand, whether I'm in the middle of a supplier meeting, or at home having dinner with the family.

3. Keep a daily diary. I find keeping a diary invaluable. At the end of *every* day, before I leave for home, I write down brief notations to record the major meetings and events of the day – a habit I've maintained for almost fifty years. I find it 'declutters' my mind, the effect almost like that of a teacher cleaning the blackboard at the end of the day. It's also proven more invaluable than mere memory (which tends to be wiped clean anyway by the new events that filter in daily!), providing me with the back-up to defend decisions that are taken and later questioned. You will never again remember in so much detail what happened on any particular day, and the peace of mind that comes with keeping an accurate record of conversations had, and decisions made, can save you time and enormous trouble. If you don't have the time or inclination to write it all down, use a Dictaphone and ask your secretary to type the notes up every morning and file them.

4. Be decisive. Every day you have to make a myriad of decisions. Don't dither. This simply defers the decision, and you will have more decisions to contend with the following day. Of course some decisions are far-reaching and require more research before reaching a conclusion, but more often than not you can rely on your gut and the split-second sense of the right thing to do. Even if it's occasionally the wrong decision, at least it was made, and events can move on.

5. Limit your evening commitments. I have to turn down a huge number of invitations to various business dinners, fundraisers and events or I'd be out almost every night. I usually limit myself by allowing business to impact on a maximum of two evenings a week.

6. Don't neglect your family. Wendy and I made up a few ground rules as we went along: one of these was that Sundays were sacrosanct. This was the day we devoted to the kids, and was when they did exactly what they pleased. I travelled every week, but always tried to be home on Mondays and Tuesdays to take the kids to school. I never missed birthdays or school plays. I was once in the process of closing an important deal when I had to announce that I needed to get to the airport, to get home for a kid's birthday. 'If you leave now, I'll give the deal to OK Bazaars,' the guy warned me. Luckily he had kids, so I could squeeze him emotionally. 'You bastard,' he finally acquiesced. 'Come back tomorrow.' And I did, clinching the site for the Norwood Hyper. Today the family still gathers almost weekly, usually on Friday nights when by and large we are all, including the grand-children, together for *shabbat*. I really value this more than anything.

7. Make time for old friends. It is easy for weeks to pass without seeing old friends, and yet see-ing old friends connects us to whom we truly are, and rejuvenates us in immeasurable ways. I have found that the easiest way to avoid neglect-ing this aspect is to have a standing 'date' with a group of friends you really value – every Monday

'It is easy for weeks to pass without seeing old friends, and yet seeing old friends connects us to whom we truly are, and rejuvenates us in immeasurable ways.'

evening, four of us get together for a game of snooker and a meal. It's very relaxing.

8. Play golf. OK, it doesn't have to be golf, but do make time for some kind of physical activity. I love golf, not only because I love the game itself but also because it creates a particular meditative state that is very useful for problem-solving. I have played at least once a week for the past forty years. Don't feel guilty if you play during the week – what is good for your mind and body must be good for business.

9. Watch TV, read, go to the movies. Escape! Switch off the Blackberry. Life is too short to spend all of it in the same reality.

10. Take an annual holiday. Once a year, really get away from everything. Switch off everything but the needs of family, and you.

And then, finally, once the day is done, and you have achieved all that the time has allowed you to, there is the great adage to take home, given to us by the humorist and consultant CW Metcalf, which needs no explanation:

PRINCIPLE #53

'Take your work seriously, but yourself lightly.'

Nuts & Bolts

Aptitude and attitude aside, there are a lot of practical, nitty-gritty aspects to starting your own business. Here, then, are a few suggested places to find useful advice, but this is just the tip – there is a wealth of information available, particularly online, so keep casting!

Getting Started

The amount of red tape involved in starting a business can be quite daunting; luckily, there are fantastic online sources packed with detailed, useful information for fledgling, inexperienced or struggling entrepreneurs. Utilise these and they will provide you with not only the answers but also the kinds of questions you need to consider. Best of all, it's free!

Three sites recommended for their authoritative, practical advice on a wide variety of entrepreneurial topics are www.southafrica.smetoolkit.org, www.bizassist.co.za and www.smallcapital.co.za. If you have time for only one, the first site ('SME toolkit', supported by the Department of Trade and Industry, the International Finance Corporation and Business Partners) is particularly comprehensive, covering absolutely everything the entrepreneur need consider, including advice on accounting and finance, business planning, marketing and sales, human resources (HR), broad-based black economic empowerment (BBBEE), legal matters, insurance, technology, operations, international business, health, and so on.

One of the first things you will have to consider, for instance, is what kind of legal entity you want to trade as, before registering your business with the Companies and Intellectual Property Registration Office (CIPRO; www.cipro.co.za). There are a number of options, but you will probably be choosing between the four described below. (There is a fifth option, the Incorporated Professional Practice, but this only applies to members of certain professions, like lawyers, doctors and accountants.) Note that it is also possible to structure your business in such a way that you can enjoy the benefits of more than one legal entity.

Whatever your personal feelings about the kind of legal entity you wish to trade as, seek professional advice before deciding on which best suits your business interests, as the decision is (or should be) fairly long term. Usually the decision to opt for one over another is due to the different tax implications, but it is also very important to take into account the number of partners and the size your operation will grow into, as well as the kind of financing you will be able to attract, the kind of administration costs involved and what would happen in the case of the business being sold or declared insolvent.

Tax guidelines for each entity change annually, depending on the directives from SARS. You can find out the latest requirements by visiting www.sars.co.za, but again I highly recommend you take advice from an accountant *as well as* a tax consultant before deciding on your legal trading entity, as most accountants are not specialised in taxation laws and regulations.

1. Close Corporation (CC): This is the most commonly used form for the start-up entrepreneur as it does not have strict auditing rules and therefore you save significantly on accounting costs. It is useful for a company owned by one person or up to ten partners. You can also change a CC to a Pty Ltd (or vice versa) at any stage.

2. Pty Limited: The Pty Ltd is useful in that it provides limited liability, i.e. creditors can only claim up to the cash total that you invested in the business and only have recourse to your personal assets if you signed surety. It also offers an easily divisible shareholding scheme, i.e. it is suitable for an investment consortium of from one to fifty owners. The downside is that there are a lot of additional accounting costs in a Pty Ltd, as you have to submit audited financial statements regardless of the size of your business. Taxation is identical to a CC.

3. Sole Proprietor: This is useful if your business does not require a large labour force and you do not envisage taking on partners (though it is possible for two or more persons to trade as a Partnership, which is similar in implications to Sole Proprietor; it usually makes more sense for partners to register a CC or Pty Ltd, especially if you are thinking big and expecting to grow turnover).

4. Trust: As the tax implications for Trusts are the most punitive, this will probably only be a consideration if you are considering the creation of a non-profit organisation, in which case special taxation benefits apply.

Tip: *If you do not have many business-related expenses, you should look into registering for the Turnover Tax for Micro Businesses, in which your turnover rather than profit is taxed, and at a far lower rate. As you do not have to provide any details of your expenses, this simplifies the paperwork hugely, but don't even think about taking this route if your business has major expenses – in which case your turnover is not much of an indication of real income! Again, understanding exactly what options exist is why it is worth speaking to a tax-savvy accountant or making an appointment with a tax consultant* before *registering your business.*

Raising Capital

Having come up with a workable business plan, realistic projections on income and expenses, and a strong, simple mission statement, let's continue as we started, and look online to explore the various ways to raise the capital. Remember: armed with a good idea and the confidence to achieve it, anything is possible, even if you have very little collateral. The three sites listed above all offer information on funding for entrepreneurs, so start by looking at these, as they may also have the most up-to-date information relevant to your business idea.

Broadly speaking, to raise capital you'll be looking at the following options:

1. Private Sector (equity funding)

Approaching an organisation devoted to assisting fledgling private enterprises with equity funding (in exchange for a return on their investment) is a good place to start. The most successful, and certainly the most established, is Business Partners (ex-Small Business Development Corporation), a specialist risk finance company for formal small and medium enterprises (www.businesspartners.co.za). The company actively supports entrepreneurial growth by providing financing, specialist sectoral knowledge and added-value services for viable small and medium businesses. Business Partners can assist start-ups with various options, such as interest-free loans for a period of time, depending on the validity of your business plan, the type of business and your understanding of the market. At the end of the interest-free loan period, you will be expected to purchase their shares at the then current value of the business, or sell the business as a whole in order to recoup their investment.

Alternatively seek your own 'angel investor' (affluent individuals or companies willing to take the risk of investing in start-up companies) – there are a number of online networks that will help facilitate this process.

If you have an aggressive business plan with an analysis of projected figures that show you can expect an above-average return on the capital invested, thanks to an interesting product or your specific expertise, you can also look at listing on the JSE in the Venture Capital Market Sector (visit www.jse.co.za). A profit history is not necessary, but you must have subscribed capital, including reserves but excluding minority interests, of at least R500 000, and not less than 1 million shares in issue.

Aside from looking for capital, look for organisations that will help to reduce your start-up costs, such as Shanduka Black Umbrellas's CSI programme (visit www.blackumbrellas.org), which offers small, medium and micro-sized (SMME) entrepreneurs an extensive working environment (office space, computers with Internet access, telephones, vehicles with drivers, a compulsory book-keeping service and a structured mentorship programme) for a nominal monthly fee.

2. Government (grants, subsidies and tax incentives)

Emerging entrepreneurs are the engine drivers of a country's economy, and as a result there are always a number of government initiatives in place to assist small enterprises with sector- and industry-specific grants.

Your first port of call should be the Department of Trade and Industry (DTI). Dig around on their website (www.dti.

gov.za) to find out what programmes are currently on offer, such as the Emerging Entrepreneur Scheme (providing loans for two to five years at nominal interest rates, as well as credit guarantees to banks). Their Enterprise Investment Programme (EIP) is an initiative offering sector-specific assistance (prior to the World Cup there was, for instance, a Tourism Support and Manufacturing Support Programme under which you could receive a maximum of 30% and minimum of 10% refund of any capital invested in the tourism or manufacturing sector).

If you have no collateral whatsoever, it is worth investigating the DTI's Khula Enterprise Finance (www.khula.org.za), which provides loan guarantees of up to 80% and risk-capital funding to entrepreneurs with no assets on a case-by-case basis, specifically to bridge the funding gap for new entrepreneurs not serviced by commercial financial institutions, who usually require surety in the form of assets.

Aside from Khula Enterprise Finance, there are a number of other development finance institutions affiliated with the DTI offering programmes that may be relevant to your business funding, such as the Industrial Development Corporation (www.idc.co.za), National Empowerment Fund (www.nefcorp.co.za) and the SA Micro-Finance Apex Fund (www.samaf.org.za).

With so many institutions and programmes floating around, and websites that are not always the most user-friendly, it may feel overwhelming trying to get a real grip on the kind of opportunities and/or tax incentives offered in your industry, not to mention the specific kind of criteria you are expected to meet, such as the Generic BEE Scorecard set out by the DTI. If so, it is worth knowing that there are companies and individuals who specialise in matching fledgling businesses with grants, loans and subsidies offered by both the government and private sector – but do make sure they are accredited by an organisation such as the Institute of Business Advisers (www.ibasa.org.za); their website also lists business advisers by region.

3. Banks (loans and collateral)

Do not be discouraged by whatever claims are made about the economic climate at any particular time: if banks are more cautious with their money, they are also more determined than ever to make more of it. A simple but well-thought-through business plan, produced by someone with relevant experience in the field, with projected figures that are market-related and sustainable, is unlikely to be turned down.

Note that there are various kinds of loans, from relatively simple business term loans (for any period but usually not longer than eight years, repayable in equal monthly instalments) to medium-term loans with flexible repayment options structured in line with cash flow and paid off over two to seven years, as well as the business revolving credit plan where, once you have paid back a portion of the loan (usually around 25%), you can withdraw the funds again, up to the original limit.

Some banks will provide a loan subject to the entrepreneur taking on a mentor for a two-year period, a cost that the bank will subsidise by 50%; this is well worth taking up.

Of course the amount you borrow is key. Ideally, the bank will require that you provide 10% of the capital, along with collateral. A 100% loan is unlikely to be offered in the current climate. However, regardless of the economic conditions – which may yet return to the buoyancy of the pre-2009 period – your maximum loan should ideally never exceed 50% of the value of the company – and even this I would find stressful.

Naturally, bankers are far more inclined to loan money when there is significant collateral – a valuable asset or assets – as guarantee or surety. If you are in the fortunate position of owning a mortgage-free house, you will be able to offer this as collateral.

However, be very cautious about making personal guarantees – particularly if you have dependants – as these inevitably endanger the security of your family. It may be a tall order, but do try your utmost to keep your business a separate entity from your personal wealth.

With this in mind, remember that the bank will not value your home as highly as your local estate agent, who is naturally inclined to optimism. If the business doesn't work out, you could be forced to make a quick sale and lose not only what you've invested in the business but a significant amount of your personal wealth.

Tip: *Most people end up opening a business account with the bank they have traditionally been associated with. Don't settle for so-called convenience. The Financial Sector Charter obliges all banks to give a certain percentage of their enterprise development funding, so it is worth shopping around to find the bank that offers you the most benefits. ABSA, for instance, runs a number of Enterprise Development Centres, located countrywide, in which start-up entrepreneurs are provided with assistance on a range of issues affecting small businesses, from devising a business plan to dealing with SARS commitments. Similarly The Business Place (www.tbp.co.za), established by Investec Bank, offers numerous practical training opportunities for SMME entrepreneurs who want to start or expand a business, and brings together business, community-based organisations and NGOs that serve a common target market. The point is that you do need to look at all the banks that offer a Small Business Development programme. That said, do stick to the well-established names – there's too much at stake to have what is effectively a business partner go bankrupt!*

Finding the Right Business or Premises

Aside from calling every agent and auction house, and exploring your designated area by car and on foot, there are a few other ways of identifying potential businesses or premises. These are described below.

1. Chamber of Commerce

Write to the local Chamber of Commerce, or to any relevant trade organisation, and find out how many similar businesses are currently registered in the area or district you are interested in. Armed with a list, you can then visit or call each one of them, doing some preliminary research into the size and nature of each organisation. Having identified those you deem suitable, you could approach the current owners and test the waters to see if, by some happy coincidence, they are ready to sell.

2. Market research

To determine where to open a store, I was taught a technique that is fairly simple but has, by and large, always produced excellent results. In essence, it involves studying the national and regional statistics produced annually by Statistics South Africa (www.statssa.gov.za) on what is being spent on food, clothing, entertainment, cars, tourism, and so on. You can compare these national statistics with the statistics of a specific town, which will enable you to identify where markets are not being adequately serviced (obviously this is easier with a defined population of a town rather than a suburb in a city).

Having compared the national statistics which show the spending patterns in a particular population (in our case, that a population of X spends Y on food sales) with a particular town's statistics, I could then determine whether this town was 'under-supermarketed', in which case the population was spending (relative to the national average) far less on food sales within the town, and a good proportion of shoppers were obviously going outside of town to purchase their groceries. You can then make an educated guess as to how the current food sales are divided between the competitors in this particular population, determine what the need is and offer a solution: you! Alternatively, the statistics may show that the town is, in fact, saturated, in which case you'll know upfront that you'll need to enter the market by pinching existing customers from competitors by offering an environment that's new and exciting and/or products that they can't purchase elsewhere.

Of course, if your business interest is more niche it will not be represented by Stats SA, in which case there are other ways to research information that may prove useful. You may, for instance, want to open an optometrist shop, in which case you will probably know the percentage of the population that needs regular eye care, and how often these customers need to revisit an optometrist. Then you need only find out how many optometrists are registered in your chosen area (again, this can be done by contacting the Chamber of Commerce or relevant trade organisation) to determine the potential need for your business. Statistically, given the size of the population in the area you are interested in, residents will either welcome a new optometrist or you will need to provide them with a service or merchandise that sets you apart from the existing optometrists.

Another potential source of information is your local town planning office, where population growth over the next five to ten years is being taken into account. Aside from looking at opportunities within existing suburbs – planning permission is needed for new roads, petrol stations, shopping centre, apartments and office blocks – newly developed suburbs need every kind of new businesses to service them.

3. Property Planning Specialists

If the idea of gathering and working with statistics to try and work out whether your business is situated in the right area is too daunting, there are a number of property specialists who can help match your business property needs with a particular area, and advise you on potential development opportunities. One of the best known is Dr Dirk Prinsloo's Urban Studies (www.urbanstudies.co.za), which can not only advise you on where, ideally, you should consider opening your business but also provides details such as how large the premises should be based on the local demographics (who shops in the area, how much disposable income, current spending patterns, etc). Another respected player in the retail property arena is Douglas Parker Associates (www.douglas-parker.co.za); the company tends to service larger clients, but produces an interesting monthly publication, *Parker Review*, which gives a precise summary of relevant articles from the top business publications, keeping you up to date with events in retail property (as well as a number of other key issues pertinent particularly to retailers). The company also produces a Towns of South Africa report, a compendium of information on each of the top 200 towns in South Africa, as well as specific Town Reports compiled from secondary data and interviews with the local authorities. You can order, or subscribe to, these publications by visiting the website and signing up.

Tip: *If you find the right premises but are unable to agree on the conditions within a formal contract, you should at least co-sign a Heads of Agreement document. This is a simple one-page document that outlines the most important points of agreement (the 'heads') of the negotiation, which are essentially:*

1. when the premises will be ready for your occupation;

2. the size of the premises;

3. a rough rental figure. If you have not as yet agreed on the figure you can state here that it will be between your figure and the landlord's figure.

Having a Heads of Agreement signed off saved me a great deal of money over the years, as it meant I had, despite the brevity of the document, legally secured the property. Note that, as the final lease is a binding contract between two parties,

---

usually with vastly different interests, it may be worth your while getting in a property specialist to assist with the final contract. You will find a number of them online.

Hiring and Firing

I highly recommend that you spend time perusing the codes and procedures found on the website of the Commission for Conciliation, Mediation and Arbitration (www.ccma.org.za). The CCMA is a dispute-resolution body established in terms of the Labour Relations Act, 66 of 1995 (LRA), and is an independent body – i.e. it does not belong to, and is not controlled by, any political party, trade union or business. As such, it is a source of invaluable information as well as practical assistance.

Certainly, if you are not in a position to hire HR assistance, and want to avoid making costly labour-related mistakes, it will be worth your while familiarising yourself with the content on the CCMA site, which includes current laws, standard employment contracts (which can be printed out and used for your business) and procedures relevant to tenders, disciplinary action, and so on. The site also lists all the CCMA offices and telephone numbers should you need specific advice on any matters.

Relations with trade unions can be difficult, but from the outset it is very important not to see the union as your enemy. Unions are by their nature adversarial, so if you set up the relationship as such this is what it will remain in perpetuity. It is far better, as an employer, to work on disarming the union, making regular contact with representatives, and following the procedures of the CCMA to the letter.

Note also that, as an employer, you will need to register with SARS (www.sars.co.za) and that the administrative burden is great (reason alone to budget for a good accountant or book-keeper), as you will need to make monthly PAYE and UIF payments and, possibly, Skills Development Levy (SDL) contributions. Penalties and interest are payable should you miss the non-negotiable deadlines for any of these compulsory monthly commitments.

Aside from considerations around character, you are well advised to be versed on the current thinking on equity, not only in terms of diversity but also disability, and get up to speed on your regional employment equity requirements. You will find these details from your local branch of the DTI, or again you can contact the CCMA.

> **Tip:** *As you probably know, even small businesses are required to have a BEE (black economic empowerment) scorecard, which measures empowerment according to the DTI's Code of Good Practice in key areas affecting Africans, Coloureds and Indians who are South African citizens. What most entrepreneurs don't realise*

is that any business with a turnover (i.e. before expenses and taxes) of R35 million or less need only comply with four of the Code's seven elements in order to procure business from the government (a big customer by anyone's book!), which in turn makes you a virtually risk-free consideration for any bank. Private companies wanting to apply for licences and concessions from the government, enter into public–private partnerships or buy state-owned assets must also comply with the Code if they wish to be considered.

Complying with four elements of the Code is far less onerous than most entrepreneurs realise, and well worth doing. Broadly, an external auditor will look at ticking four of the following elements:

Ownership: *what percentage of your business is owned by a black person(s)?*

Management at senior level: *how much of the day-to-day control is managed by black person(s)?*

Employment equity: *how fair is your human resource development? How diverse/representative is your workforce? (Other minority groups, such as those with disabilities, are included.)*

Skills development: *what initiatives do you have in place to develop skills within your workforce?*

> **Preferential procurement:** *what percentage of your suppliers is non-white/from previously disadvantaged groups?*
>
> **Enterprise development:** *is your business creating/supporting/developing other sustainable small businesses?*
>
> **Corporate social investment:** *are you investing time or money in community-related issues and charities?*
>
> Note that different industries are required to draw up their own charters on BEE, so that all sectors can adopt a uniform approach to empowerment and how it is measured. For more information on black economic empowerment, visit the DTI website.

Keeping Abreast*

Regardless of your particular business, it is essential that you keep abreast of general economic trends, and set aside at least thirty minutes a day for this. Aside from reading the local business papers, there are a plethora of online options, from local sources such as the *Financial Mail* (www.fm.co.za) and *Business Day* (www.businessday.co.za) to international CNN or Sky News updates. However, with so much online choice, some people are better served by carefully selecting and following the opinions of a few independent writers. Almost every industry has its choice thinkers, but if you are at all affected by the financial markets it is worth subscribing to Richard Russell's www.dowtheoryletters.com; born in 1924, Russell is that rare writer: able to fully contextualise current events, having lived through the Great Depression, the Second World War and all the other boom-and-bust periods, and writing incisively about the stock market since the late 1950s. Also worth mentioning are Bloomberg's Caroline Baum and John Mauldin; the latter has over one million subscribers, and he summarises current events in the context of economic theory. Mauldin also posts a regular 'Outside the Box' letter, bringing together various experts' topical research on the events of the day; it costs nothing to subscribe and is well worth it (www.2000wave.com).

An inspiring website worth visiting on a regular basis is www.ted.com: aptly billed as 'riveting talks by remarkable people', it offers a philosophical take on a broad range of subjects, from business and technology to design and global issues. The speakers are as diverse as the topics, and include the likes of Bill Gates, Jamie Oliver, Peter Eigen, Malcolm Gladwell, Richard Dawkins and JK Rowling.

To better understand the specific market you are serving, it's also worth keeping up to date with international research; one such site is www.researchandmarkets.com, billed as the world's largest market research resource, with reports on every conceivable service and product category across many countries.

* Please note website are subject to change.

And Finally

As I said at the beginning, this is by no means a comprehensive list of resources; just keep looking, keep gathering –
remember, sometimes all it takes to land a big catch is a tiny
sprat.

Given that a business requires meticulous and ongoing research, it is finally time for me to hand over to you.

It is my fervent wish that you put this book down feeling
more than ever ready to tackle the admirable task of running
your own business, master of your destiny. Good luck!